Struggle and Suffrage in Peterborough

This book is dedicated to my mother, Dorothy. It is thanks to her, and the childhood experiences she gave me, that I have such an interest in history today.

Struggle and Suffrage in Peterborough

Women's Lives and the Fight for Equality

Abigail Hamilton-Thompson

AN IMPRINT OF PEN & SWORD BOOKS LTD.
YORKSHIRE – PHILADELPHIA

First published in Great Britain in 2022 by
Pen & Sword History
An imprint of
Pen & Sword Books Ltd
Yorkshire – Philadelphia

Copyright © Abigail Hamilton-Thompson, 2022

ISBN 978 1 52671 672 9

The right of Abigail Hamilton-Thompson to be identified as Author of this work has been asserted by her in accordance with the Copyright, Designs and Patents Act 1988.

A CIP catalogue record for this book is available from the British Library.

All rights reserved. No part of this book may be reproduced or transmitted in any form or by any means, electronic or mechanical including photocopying, recording or by any information storage and retrieval system, without permission from the Publisher in writing.

Typeset in Times New Roman 11.5/14
by SJmagic DESIGN SERVICES, India.
Printed and bound in the UK by CPI Group (UK) Ltd.

Pen & Sword Books Limited incorporates the imprints of Atlas, Archaeology, Aviation, Discovery, Family History, Fiction, History, Maritime, Military, Military Classics, Politics, Select, Transport, True Crime, Air World, Frontline Publishing, Leo Cooper, Remember When, Seaforth Publishing, The Praetorian Press, Wharncliffe Local History, Wharncliffe Transport, Wharncliffe True Crime and White Owl.

For a complete list of Pen & Sword titles please contact
PEN & SWORD BOOKS LIMITED
47 Church Street, Barnsley, South Yorkshire, S70 2AS, England
E-mail: enquiries@pen-and-sword.co.uk
Website: www.pen-and-sword.co.uk

Or
PEN AND SWORD BOOKS
1950 Lawrence Rd, Havertown, PA 19083, USA
E-mail: Uspen-and-sword@casematepublishers.com
Website: www.penandswordbooks.com

Contents

Introduction — vii

Chapter One Famous women of Peterborough — 1

Chapter Two Education in Peterborough — 9

Chapter Three Working in Peterborough — 20

Chapter Four Home life in Peterborough — 38

Chapter Five Women and the Wars — 45

Chapter Six Health and Poverty in Peterborough — 55

Chapter Seven Women's Leisure Time in Peterborough — 71

Chapter Eight Active Citizens in Peterborough — 86

Afterword — 116

Bibliography — 117

Index — 120

Introduction

This book explores the lives of women in Peterborough between 1850 and 1950, and considers the way in which different aspects of those lives changed over the years: education, home life, work, heath & poverty, leisure activities, suffrage and active citizens. It will also consider the ways in which both the First and Second World Wars affected the citizens in Peterborough, including the loss of so many men from the community and the lifestyle changes that had to be made as part of the war effort.

Women in Peterborough experienced a good deal of change during this time. Provision for the poor increased with an ever expanding workhouse in Thorpe Road and Miss Pear's Almshouses, which replaced a smaller almshouse in Cumbergate in 1903. Health care improved with a small infirmary in Priestgate and then the city's first operating theatre was attached to said infirmary. Schooling became available to all girls in the city when education became compulsory in Britain, replacing the various privately run dame schools dotted around Peterborough and when the First World War arrived, women were required to replace men in the workforce and this continued well into the Second World War whereby women were very much active citizens in and around Peterborough. Let us not forget that this period was not always a joyous one for women in Peterborough as during the First World War more than one thousand men from the town died leaving whole communities of mothers, wives and children distraught particularly as a number of these men signed up together in the same Pals battalions and fought/died together in the same battles. A working class wife was responsible for keeping her family as clean, warm and dry as possible in housing stock that was literally rotting around them as well as potentially supplement the family's income by taking on extra work on top of her domestic duties.

CHAPTER ONE

Famous women of Peterborough

Edith Cavell 1865-1915

There are a number of notable Peterborough women commemorated within the cathedral in the city centre, including Edith Cavell, a British nurse shot by the Germans during the First World War, who has a Blue memorial plaque on a cathedral pillar. Edith Cavell was born to a vicar in Swardeston, Norfolk, on 4 December 1865 and was a pupil-teacher of Laurel Court. Thanks to her former employer's, Margaret Gibson, connections in Belgium, Edith was offered a job as a governess to a family in Brussels where she stayed for five years before returning home to nurse her sick father. This may well have given her the inspiration to train as a nurse at the Royal London Hospital in London. Nurse Edith Cavell was executed by German firing squad on 12 October 1915 while working in Belgium helping injured soldiers; she had been accused of being a spy and of helping over 200 Allied soldiers to escape. Initially buried where she was shot, her family subsequently requested that she be reburied at Norwich Cathedral. The news of her death was received with both sorrow and outrage by the citizens of Peterborough, and both King George V and King Albert of Belgium paid tribute to her. Edith is remembered within Peterborough by the naming of a city-centre car park and Peterborough's Hospital, but mainly there is also a memorial to her in the cathedral which was paid for by donations collected from friends, pupils and former teachers from Laurel Court School. The Blue Irish plaque reads:

> Right dear in the sight of the
> Lord is the death of His Saints
> In thankful remembrance of the
> Christian example of
> Edith Louisa Cavell
> who devoted her life to nursing
> the sick and for helping Belgian
> French and British soldiers to
> escape was on October 12th 1915
> put to death by the Germans
> at Brussels where she had
> nursed their wounded this
> Tablet was placed here by the
> Teachers Pupils and Friends
> of her old School in
> Laurel Court

****

Katherine of Aragon, 1845-1536

Katherine of Aragon, first wife of Henry VIII, is buried here. Initially married to Prince Arthur, the elder son of Henry VII and Henry VIII's elder brother, she was born in Spain but moved to England for her marriage. Upon Arthur's death, she went on to marry his younger brother. They were married for 24 years but Katherine failed to provide a male heir and, upon her famous divorce in 1533, ended up being banished to Kimbolton Castle, some twenty miles from Peterborough, dying there on 7 January 1536 aged 50. It was said that the Fenland climate damaged her health and contributed towards her death. The cathedral hosts an annual Tudor themed festival dedicated to Katherine's memory, usually held at the end of January, to commemorate her burial within the Cathedral on 29 January 1536, which Henry VIII did not attend. Her funeral procession between Kimbolton Castle, via Sawtry Abbey, was recreated in 1986 to mark the 450th anniversary of her death. This festival usually lasts a couple of days and includes a special memorial service to the Queen's memory during which there is a laying of a wreath by representatives from the Spanish Embassy. Katherine of Aragon's grave is rarely seen without flowers or pomegranates, her chosen symbol – a painful one as pomegranates represent fertility and the only surviving child of her union with Henry VIII was a daughter, the Princess Mary. The coat of arms above her grave in the cathedral is that of Wales and Spain hence Peterborough's twinning with Alcara de Henares, Katherine of Aragon's place of birth.

Lastly, in the south transept of Peterborough Cathedral, there is a chapel dedicated to three royal women; Cynesburga, Cyneswitha and kinswoman Tibba. Within the chapel is a monument carved in the eighteenth century with a mish-mash of medieval nichery, which is supposedly the shrine of St Tibba. Cyneburga and Cyneswitha, also known as Kyneburga and Kyneswitha, were both daughters of Penda, King of Mercia. The sisters converted to Christianity against their father's wishes and Cyneburga subsequently founded an abbey at Castor in the Soke of Peterborough. Cyneburga died on 15 September in AD 680 and became revered as a Saint. Her remains as well as those of her sister Cyneswitha and kinswoman Tibba were moved to Peterborough Abbey and then later transferred to Thorny Abbey. Cyneburga, Cyneswitha and Tibba are commemorated by a chapel in the Cathedral and there is a uniquely named twelfth-century parish church of St Kyneburga in Castor. Saint Kyneburga has a legend attached to her which tells how she escaped from three men who intended to harm her. Kyneburga prayed for help and a pit opened up which swallowed the men who were following her, the path that she took as she escaped was covered with flowers. Kyneburga escaped safely and become devoted to God.

Mary Queen of Scots was also buried at the Cathedral for 25 years after her execution on 8 February 1587 in the Great Hall of Fotheringhay Castle near Oundle, but the former Queen was disinterred in 1612 at the request of her son King James VI and I, thus relocating her remains to an ornate marble tomb in Westminster Abbey.

Gladys Benstead, 1896-mid 1960s

Gladys was the first woman to work as a railway clerk outside of London and became a negotiator for women's wages in the National Union of Railwaymen in the 1920s. It was very unusual for a woman to hold a position of this type in the trade union movement at this time and such a role really was a huge step in the role of women's rights. During the Second World War, Gladys served on the Standing Committee of Working Women Organisations and on the Fuel Advisory Committee under William Beveridge where she assisted with fuel rationing. In 1926 Gladys was elected as President of the NUR Midland District Women's Guild, as agreed by a majority of attendees. She was elected as a Labour councillor to Peterborough City Council in 1944. Her husband, John, was elected as the general secretary of the NUR and in 1946 he received an OBE. Gladys had lived in Peterborough off and on during her life before becoming Mayor of Peterborough in 1955.

Katherine Clayton, 1843-1933

Katherine's father was Thomas Hare, a Liberal reformer and barrister. He had held the position of the Inspector of Charities and had become involved with the call for women's suffrage, thus speaking at public meetings in aid of the cause and joining campaign groups. Katherine, naturally influenced by her father, also became involved in the campaign and started signing petitions that were sent to Parliament in 1866. In 1872, she married Lewis Clayton, who later became the Bishop of Peterborough, and she continued her involvement in the votes for women campaign. In 1896, she signed a memorandum to Sir Arthur Balfour, the Conservative party leader, requesting that the government gave some time to discuss this Women's Suffrage in Parliament. Katherine also attended local meetings dedicated to women's suffrage, along with her daughter, Kitty, and attended the 'at home' meeting with Emmeline Pankhurst at the Angel Hotel. Katherine campaigned to raise money to replace the marble tomb of Katherine of Aragon at Peterborough cathedral (as a former bishop had used the previous memorial in his conservatory). She contacted other wealthy ladies with the same first name and asked them to donate resulting in the lovely tomb you can see today. Katherine was also awarded an OBE for her campaigns around education.

Louise Creighton, 1850-1936

The wife of Mandell Creighton, also a Bishop of Peterborough, Louise was a Victorian social reformer and a president of the National Council of Women Workers, which she set up in 1885. This was to co-ordinate the voluntary efforts of women across Great Britain. In 1890 Louise and another lady founded the Ladies Dining Society, a private dining and discussion club for ladies. Many of the members were associated with Newnham College, one of the first Cambridge colleges offering university level education to women. Whilst living in Peterborough, Louise invited the group to meet in Peterborough several times to continue their private women's dining and discussion club. Louise and her husband spent only a short time in Peterborough between 1891 and 1897 but Louise was a huge influence on Katherine Clayton. Louise set up a Peterborough branch of the Mothers' Union, of which Katherine was secretary. The organisation's motto is 'For home and family'. Whilst both women were very socially active, Louise rebuked the Suffrage cause until after her husband had died in 1906.

Florence Saunders 1855-1904

The youngest daughter of Augustus Page Saunders, Dean of Peterborough Cathedral between 1853 and 1878, Florence was considered Peterborough's equivalent of the famous nurse, Florence Nightingale. As a child, Florence had accompanied her father on many visits to the sick and poor people living in the Boongate (roughly where Eastgate is now) area of Peterborough. At the time, provision for poor people was available via either the workhouse or infirmary; there was no nursing care available in the nineteenth century unless you could afford to pay for it. Florence was initially taught at home by her father before attending the Laurel Court school run by Miss Gibson and Miss Van Dissel. Once she was of age, Florence joined the Evelina Hospital for Sick Children in London to study nursing. After completing her training, she returned to Peterborough to care for the sick. In 1884 Florence founded the Peterborough District Nursing Association at her own home – St Oswald's Close, to allow people to be cared for in their own homes by nurses who were supervised by a superintendent. She then took on further training in hospital administration skills at the John Radcliffe Infirmary in Oxford. Florence was also an enthusiastic pioneer of the Northamptonshire County Nursing Association which was set up not long after a public meeting, recorded in the *Northamptonshire Mercury*, 30 January 1903. Miss Saunders was then the honorary secretary of the proposed association, despite her failing health. She said that 'there could be no doubt in the mind of anyone as to the need, the increasing need, for nurses ministering to the sick poor. The ignorance of the poor upon the simplest hygiene principles such as cleanliness, ventilation, and the common-sense requirements of patients was appalling; in fact, she believed that there was in consequence not only unnecessary suffering and permanent affliction, but even loss of life.' An important part of this proposed scheme would be to get young women of the county to become district nurses as there was a lack of nurses particularly in the Peterborough area.

Florence died on 12 April 1904 at the age of just 48; her obituary in the *Peterborough Advertiser* read: 'Notwithstanding the fact that her duties as Superintendent occupied most of her time, Miss Saunders never gave up her active work of visiting, soothing and healing, almost to the last she moved about in the much loved uniform among her humble friends.'

Lily Hodgson (birth/death unknown)

Formerly of Peterborough Infirmary and originally from Ryhope Colliery area in Sunderland, Nurse Lily was attached to the Isle of Wight Field Hospital during the First World War, working on the French/Belgian battlefields near Dunkirk.

She wrote home to say:

> I had no time to come home after we left Antwerp. They were so busy at Calais that we went there. The wounded were coming in thick and fast, and there was no one there to attend to them. We arrived there at the end of September and stayed a fortnight till we patched them and sent them to England.
>
> We then got word that they wanted help at (deleted by the censor), so we arrived there on 9th November, and the night I arrived I went down to the railway sheds at 9 p.m. where the wounded trains were arriving, and I worked there until 8 a.m. the next day, and I have done the same ever since.
>
> We used to get as many as 800 or 900 a night – Algerians, Senegalese, Turcos and French, straight from the firing line. Poor things, they were so patient and grateful. Some of them had not had the dressing done for five or six days, and it was painful to see them, and such dreadful wounds. It is very hard work, but still it is good work, and I don't mind in the least what I do for them. We have also got a nice hospital at, (censor deleted), right on the sea front, and we send most of the cases up there. You would like to see the wards, indeed I would like to send a photo of them, and I will when I can.
>
> I went out to the front the other day with the ambulance and the doctors. I took some shirts, cigarettes and matches to the men in the

trenches, which they were delighted to get. I am afraid to say tears stand in my eyes to hear the heroes say 'An angel in white, English mademoiselle'. We are still waiting for the kaiser to arrive in Calais and Dunkirk, where he will get a grand reception both by sea and land and all.

Lily also reported on a home visit that she had had narrow escapes from German bombs and the hospital she worked at in the Malo les Bains area suffered broken windows.

****

CHAPTER TWO

Education in Peterborough

At the start of 1850, very little evidence exists in terms of the dame schools and private schools in the Peterborough area, which girls could attend, as education was limited. Dame schools were small groups of 10 or 12 boys and girls taught in the front room of a cottage by the home owner, usually a woman. The dame schools often had a poor reputation and were usually nothing more than a cheap form of daycare as the women running them typically had little or no qualifications. They may have taught reading and writing to a rudimentary level, charging between 3d and 4d per pupil per week. In 1851 female literacy rates were at 55 per cent whereas men were much higher at 70 per cent. More substantial ventures whose names appeared in local directories, such as Elizabeth and Susannah Whitwell ran schools, including boarding schools, that were aimed at middle class pupils, mainly girls. These schools were more likely to teach painting and fancy needlework rather than the Three R's of the elementary schools. Mrs Barber, the wife of the Headmaster of the Deacon's School, ran a boarding school which still existed in 1902 and Mrs Edwards of the Crescent had an advertisement for a school in 1876.

Elizabeth and Susannah Whitwell were the two sisters of John, a leading figure within the Peterborough community, and ran a school for ladies in Narrow Bridge Street, the same street where their other brother Thomas conducted his business. Their school was listed in the Post Office Directory of 1847. John Whitwell, the brother was a driving force in assisting Peterborough to gain its Charter of Incorporation in 1874 with the municipal borough now under the government of a mayor, six aldermen and eighteen councillors.

A notice appeared in the *Peterborough Advertiser* on 14 July 1855 announcing a new school in town:

> The MISSES STRICKLAND RESPECTFULLY inform their Friends and the Public that they intend opening a School after the Midsummer Vacation for the instruction of young Ladies. With hopeful confidence they solicit a share of public patronage, assuring their friends that every effort will be used for advancement of the pupils entrusted to their charge. The First Quarter will commence on Monday July 16th 1855. TERMS – Young Ladies are Boarded and Instructed in Writing, Arithmetic, Geography, History, etc at £18 18s per annum. Day Pupils 10s 6d per Quarter. Laundress: Two Guineas per annum. Each young lady to be provided with a pair of sheets, a Fork and spoon, which will be returned on their leaving. A Quarter's Notice previous to the removal of a young lady. 34 Cowgate Street, Peterborough.

In the nineteenth century, there was an important development in the provision of universal free education for children and as such the British and Foreign School Society set up free British schools and teacher training based on non-sectarian principles. In many places these schools were active rivals of the established Church schools such as the National schools founded in the nineteenth century by the National Society for Promoting Religious Education. These schools provided elementary education, in accordance to the teachings of the Church of England, to the children of the poor. The National Society was established in 1811 to set up schools based on the system introduced by Andrew Bell, a Scottish Episcopalian priest and educationalist. Its aim was to establish a National School in every single parish in England and Wales, with schools usually built next to and named after the parish church. Together with the British and Foreign School Society, formed in 1814, the two provided the first national system of elementary education within England and Wales. The schools eventually were absorbed into the state system, either as fully state run schools or as faith schools run by the state.

Elementary education in Peterborough was largely non-denominational, and generally was the main choice for parents moving into the city. In 1850 a British and Foreign Society non-conformist school could be found in the Congregational Chapel at the corner of Wood Street and Westgate but it soon found the premises too small, with the boys moving out to a new school in New Road in 1859 and the infants and girls remaining in the chapel.

The Fitzwilliam and Castor Infant Schools provided elementary state education for most of the children in Castor, Ailsworth, Upton and Sutton and, occasionally, Castor Mills and Milton Park. Each child enjoyed a great deal of support in the form of funding, prizes and treats from some of the residents of the 'big' houses and farms – including those living at Castor House, the Cedars, Upton Manor, Sutton Grange, Ailsworth Manor Farm and the Fitzwilliam family of Milton.

Peterborough town was divided into two parishes; St Mark's and St Mary's, and each parish opened their own school in 1857. St Mary's built their school next to the church whereas St Mark's opened their school initially in temporary quarters, in a building provided by the railway company in New England. Permanent premises were erected on the same estate in 1864. The school was enlarged twice, in 1874 and 1876, before the boys were moved to a separate school on Walpole Street in 1891. The entire school was transferred to the new Council School on Lincoln Road in 1902. The first elementary day school was the 'National' in Nelson Street, now lost to the Queensgate shopping centre. The National school was recorded in the Northampton Post Office Directory of 1847 as having 144 girls on its books as well as 373 boys and then later in 1890, it had 228 boys and 173 girls attending. The elementary day school was run under the rules of the Reverend Weddred and the committee were local supporters of the National Society for the Education of the Children of the Poor in the Principles of the Church of England. Sunday attendance at the local church was important but this rule could be interpreted generously as in other towns with National schools. A Board of Education grant, around 1890, was made available to the school so that colour washing could be done and a ceiling given to the boys' classroom which at the time was open to the slates, but the girls and infants had to wait until the following year for their classroom to be updated. Later, in 1898, the school was referred to as 'well lighted and giving eight square foot per child', but was subsequently closed in 1924.

St Mark's parish was divided in 1869 and subsequently built new schools within its parish on Gladstone Road. The new parish of St John's, despite having the existing 'National' school inside its boundary, also set up a parish school in Albert Street which grew to a register of over 900 children within the three departments. The British Society set up a school in Oundle Road in 1855 and opened two schools for girls and infants: Millfield in St Martin's Street and the Methodist schoolroom in Cobden Street. All of these schools were later integrated into the new city schools. Neighbouring parishes of Werrington and Woodston opened schools in 1859 and 1871. The National Society opened at Dogsthorpe in 1852 and Newark in 1872

At a meeting in 1860 for The National Society for Promoting the Education of the Poor in the Principles of the Established Church, the Dean of Peterborough Cathedral spoke of the need for a girls' school. Extra money was needed to fund this school and the most viable suggestions made were either to share the current contributions, or to ask subscribers to donate more money. A committee was formed, which included the Dean, to plan and ensure the establishment of a new school.

The 1870 Education Act, also known as the Forster Act after its sponsor William Forster, was the first piece of legislation that dealt specifically with the provision of education in England and Wales and showed a commitment to providing education between the ages of 5 and 10. However, between 1870 and 1891, parents had to pay fees to have their child educated. In 1893 the compulsory attendance was raised to 11 and in 1899 to 12. The city rejected the idea of a school board under the 1870 Act as it felt that the voluntary schools were fulfilling all needs, but did instead form a School Attendance Board to ensure full attendance of all children between 5 and 14 years of age. Labour certificates could be granted to those children aged 11 and over who had attained a set standard of education and therefore could be released from school for full employment. The attendance officer also regulated half-timers. In 1870 when the government took on responsibility for elementary education with the Elementary Education Act of 1870, the British Schools turned into locally administered board schools. The Act also provided for the establishment of board schools to supplement the busy society schools; this allowed for funding of 50 per cent of the running costs but not capita; funding. The National Society was able to raise £10 million nationally and to almost double the number of National Schools across the parishes over the next fifteen years. However, running costs mounted up and many of these were either closed or were forced to hand over to school boards. The Education Acts of 1875 and 1880 made school attendance compulsory and as such this made all of the Peterborough schools overcrowded. In 1902, a new Education Act drafted by Arthur Balfour (who later became Prime Minister) radically reorganised the administration of education at local levels. All school boards were abolished and all elementary schools were now managed by the local education authorities until control by the councils. These councils were encouraged to provide free secondary education places for working-class children. In 1906 free school meals were provided as it was found that over a third of children nationally were malnourished, and in the following year medical inspections of children were introduced. Then, 1908, the school leaving age was increased to 14 and all secondary fees were abolished in state education. In 1944 free secondary education was introduced for all pupils and a three tiered system was introduced for secondary aged children: grammar, secondary modern and technical, the leaving age was also raised to 15.

Peterscourt, formerly known as St Peter's College, on City Road is a fine piece of Victorian architecture which still survives today. Built between 1856–64 as a teacher's training college on behalf of the Diocese of Peterborough, the building was designed by Sir Richard Gilbert Scott, most noted for the Albert Memorial and the Midland Grand Hotel which fronts St Pancras Railway Station in London, in the gothic style with red and blue bricks. St Peter's was originally used as a male teacher training college until 1914, when the outbreak of the First World War caused the number of students to fall dramatically and closure became inevitable. The building reopened as a women's teacher training college in 1921, but closed a few years later in the mid 1930s owing to the shortage of finance. A small school was built alongside the college to provide practice for the teachers but this has now been replaced by a modern office block and Peterscourt is now used as offices.

At the time of the 1881 census the master and matron of the workhouse were Mr and Mrs Poppleworth and Mr and Mrs Lyle were the schoolmaster and schoolmistress. There were 200 residents listed. In 1882, the workhouse guardians were asked by the Local Government Board to sign a memorial which was in support of an enquiry into the education and care of pauper children. In an edition of the *Standard*, John Whitwell had suggested that while workhouse schools were good, he believed that the children who attended in large numbers became hardened and corrupted. At the beginning of 1883 the guardians had agreed to six boys and four girls being boarded out (to arrange for a person to stay with someone who is paid to look after them for a period of time – nowadays fostering). Two couples, both equally qualified, were being considered to take on the role of a new schoolmaster and mistress. These were Mr and Mrs Sheard from Epping and Mr and Mrs Nuttall from Maidstone. The Nuttalls were appointed and, unusually, were allowed to bring their children to live with them in the workhouse; this naturally evoked criticism. The Local Government Board changed their mind about this decision and informed the workhouse board that the Nuttalls could not have their children live with them. It was then discovered that the Nuttalls had actually been dismissed from their previous posts at Maidstone due to 'some punishment administered to girls [which] caused an enquiry', but the Nuttalls still took up their posts at the Peterborough workhouse without their children and with approval from the Local Government Board.

Mrs Margaret Gibson was made an Honorary Freewoman of the City of Peterborough on 11 November 1926, her 90th birthday. She was the first woman to receive this honour 'in recognition of her long and distinguished services to the city in the cause of education of girls'. The mayor at the time, John Thomas Fisher, JP (1926-1927), said: 'It would be impossible for the City to find a lady more deserving or fitting on who to bestow this great honour, whose whole life and work have been devoted to the benefit and instruction of others.'

With her friend, Miss Annette Van Dissel, Margaret Gibson opened a school at Laurel Court in 1870. An advertisement in the 1884 Peterborough Directory for the Laurel Court House Girls' School states that:

> The aim of this school is to give a high moral training, offering to the pupils the advantages of home life. French and German are the languages of the house. Especial attention is paid to the culture of Music. Pupils are prepared for the Cambridge and Oxford examinations. Fees are 60 Guineas per Annum, paid in advance and a terms notice is required before the removal of a pupil.

Margaret Gibson was born on 11 November 1837 at Mallow in County Cork, Ireland, to an Irish clergyman. When she was 12, her family moved to Monkstown, Dublin, after the devastation of the potato famine, as her father took on the role of military chaplaincy. In 1853 Margaret moved to London and took on social work roles. At the age of 31 she moved to Holland and worked; this is where she met Miss Annette Van Dissel, who became her lifelong friend and confidant. They decided to open a school in England, and after Miss Gibson heard Bishop Magee speak at Peterborough Cathedral, she decided that the city was perfect for their needs. The school first opened at 2 South View, London Road in 1869, but, within a year, soon relocated to Laurel Court in the cathedral cloisters after buying out the owner, Mrs Freeman. Laurel Court school quickly became very popular due to eminent individuals such as the Earl of Chichester, Mrs Magee (the Bishop's wife) and Lady Barrington of Hampshire, providing references for the school. Pupils who attended were often daughters of clergymen and professional men. It was said that Miss Gibson was a formidable character, running the school with a firm hand; she was known to take an evening walk around the cathedral grounds dressed in a long black dress, white stockings and a white muslin cap. Young ladies who had finished at Laurel Court could find work by placing an ad in the newspapers such as this one in the Morning Post on 21 November 1907 – 'Young GERMAN lady of good family REQUIRES a PLACE to teach Music and German in a good family. – Answer Frl. Marie Tungck, care of Miss Gibson, Laurel Court House, Peterborough.'

However, despite Miss Gibson's eccentric tendencies, she took an interest in her pupils, offering help and support long after they had graduated from the school. Miss Gibson died on 12 April 1928, aged 91.

Annette Van Dissel, the other half of the school's partnership, was less renowned. Annette was the daughter of a Dutch clergyman and also carried out translation work for magazines as she was proficient in French, Italian, Swedish, German and Spanish. She tutored Edith Cavell in French and was said to have a kind, gentle disposition. Annette passed away in 1914 aged 73.

A rival to Laurel Court was the High School for Girls at 198 Park Road near Huntly Grove. 198 Park Road was originally built for Henry Hicks, a local builder and brickmaker. Founded as a day school for girls in 1895, the private school was run by a Miss May Hill with the help of her sister Annie. Although Annie died in 1907, Miss May continued to run the school, which was gaining in acclaim until she retired in 1919 with Miss Amy Mansfield as her successor. Although the school closed at the end of the Easter term in 1935, the school was relocated to its present site in 1936 and opened renaming itself as Westwood House with Miss Helen Belgion as headmistress. It is a Woodard school, a member of the largest collection of independent Church of England Schools in

England and Wales, formerly known as the Society of St Nicholas and aligned with the work of Nathaniel Woodard, a Church of England priest. 198 Park Road, after the school moved, then became the Post Office Telephone School and the Manager's Office until the 1980s.

In 1902 Peterborough became a Part III Authority so was now responsible for elementary education and the County Council took over responsibility for secondary and elementary education in the Peterborough and Barnack Rural Districts. The County School for Girls was established in 1902 to train pupil-teachers at the County Technical School in Broadway from the ages of 14 onwards for two years full time, then a further two years part time, followed by a studentship to complete their training. The school, which was to become Peterborough County Grammar School, opened in 1904 with ninety-nine pupils. Miss Wragge from Oxford became Head, and Miss Hough, also from Oxford, was one of the main teachers. In 1907, the school first relocated to the former Free Library in Park Road and opened its doors to girls of all academic ability. This was a temporary measure until the new buildings were ready for use in 1911, when it relocated again to the present site in Lincoln Road, where it was opened by the Marchioness of Exeter. There was a Junior school opposite with six large additional classrooms and a cloakroom. The school motto was 'Non Sibi Sed Deo et Alteri' (not for oneself but for God and others). The uniform comprised of navy hat-bands bearing the initials of PTC and the motto around the initials in red. The pupils were greatly daring by wearing navy gym suits with knee length shorts and tunics as opposed to the ankle length skirts that were worn by other schools locally. In the summer term of 1908, ten girls were entered for the Oxford Senior Examination and all ten passed with six gaining honours. The school raised money for the Red Cross during the First World War and both pupils and teachers knitted socks to send to the soldiers fighting in France. During this time pupils living out of town found it difficult to travel between home and school so both Miss Wragge and Miss Hough found permission to obtain a school boarding house in the empty St Peter's College (all of the male students had enlisted in the war). Post war, St Peter's College reopened and, as such, the boarding house was transferred to 'The Lawns' in Thorpe Road.

The school, its pupils, families and former pupils were well known for fundraising in order to improve the facilities on site. The school swimming pool was opened in June 1930 at a cost of £1,563, entirely paid for by fundraising. A hard tennis court was put in at a cost of £100 in 1933 followed by the library in 1936 at a cost of £420. Each table and chair within the library were all marked with the names of those who donated money. During the Second World War, the two school magazines, the Chronicle and Old Girls, were discontinued, with the money that would have been spent in producing the Old Girls sheets being donated to a relief fund started by the secondary schools of England to provide an ambulance. The pupils of the County Secondary School for Girls demonstrated a generous nature by renting, equipping and maintaining a refugee hostel in Cromwell Road during the First World War for the Belgians. The expenses of the Belgian family living here were met weekly by school contributions. Before long, a second property was sourced in Alma Road. The girls regularly visited the hostels to play with the Belgian children and often took them to their own homes for tea.

In 1920, a pupil of the school gained a State Scholarship, an extremely valuable university scholarship. In 1921, the school topped the list of girls' schools in the Oxford Higher Certificate of Education and later became a grammar school. This was an external examination – the School Certificate was achievable at 16 and the Higher School Certificate at 18. In the 1926 Chronicle news it was reported that there were twenty-six girls in the Upper V form, aged sixteen, that were about to take their Oxford School Certificate examination. When Miss Wragge and Miss Hough retired in 1936, the school had nearly 500 pupils. It was demolished in the 1980s to build Lincoln's Court, a block of warden controlled flats.

Under the Butler Education Act of 1944 which resulted in the abolition of school fees, many schools within Peterborough became voluntary aided or voluntary controlled primary schools which were funded by the state but still able to promote the teachings of the Church of England. The County School for Girls renamed itself and became known as the Peterborough County Grammar School for Girls.

The 1918 Act raised the school leaving age from 12 years to 14 years but there were exemptions for those who found suitable employment. However, these exemptions were abolished in 1921. It was rare for girls to carry on in education past the legal school leaving age. According to the County Girls Chronicle, in 1924, three girls achieved open scholarships. These were to attend Girton College in Cambridge, Oxford University and the Royal Holloway College. In the late Victorian era most universities became available to women apart from Oxford until 1920 and Cambridge in 1948.

CHAPTER THREE

Working in Peterborough

In the nineteenth century, British women were expected to marry and have children. However there was, in fact, a shortage of men. The mortality rate for boys was far higher than for girls; a large number of males served in the armed forces abroad and men were more likely to emigrate than women. The laws in Britain were based on the idea that women would get married and that their husbands would take care of them.

Before the passing of the 1882 Married Property Act, when a woman got married, her wealth was passed on to her husband and if she continued to work, all of her money would go to him. Upper and middle class women were more dependent on men than a working class woman; they were dependent on their fathers until they got married and, once married, it was extremely difficult to get a divorce or even separate. The Matrimonial Causes Act of 1857 gave men the right to divorce their wives on the grounds of adultery, however, married women were unable to obtain a divorce if they discovered that their husbands had been unfaithful. To remain single was thought to be a disgrace and, at thirty, an unmarried woman was called an old maid. After a single woman's parents died, what could they do and where could they go? To live with your brother could be a somewhat awkward burden and it was difficult to find work other than as a governess which was a role with difficult conditions and a low salary. The Married Women's Property Act removed the restrictions that wealthy married women had from controlling their own property and gave them equal status with their husbands and their own property rights.

Many lower class women in Victorian Britain assisted their families by taking on wage paying jobs alongside their already heavy domestic burdens. At this time birth rates were high and life expectancy was improving and, as such, Victorian families were generally large. Residential domestic service and the increasing trend of taking on lodgers meant that many households became swollen in size. Some households now included grandparents who assisted with childcare, particularly when the mothers were working outside of the home. Many young women migrated to towns and cities in search of work as agricultural employment opportunities declined, and it was easier to find accommodation if it was offered alongside a job.

Some women and girls added to their family's income by taking on either intermittent or low paid work in comparison to their male counterparts. The male breadwinner wage was generally regarded as an ideal or norm, but in practice many households were very much dependent on female earnings, particularly any households run by widows. New technologies and patterns of work offered many opportunities for females, despite the regulation of hours and conditions of work for women and girls, as we shall see below. Thus the majority of women in Victorian society in the lower classes worked for wages.

There is however an absence of reliable information regarding women's work. The most obvious source of information are the census enumerators' books where occupations were included. But, women's work was often misclassified, and part-time or casual labour was not regarded as important enough to declare. Alternatively, a woman's occupation may have been illegal as is the case with prostitution or working in illegal sweat shops; or they may have preferred to have kept their income a secret from their husband. The survival of wage books is poor and trade directories were published irregularly – these only record the names of business proprietors. Home based work could include finishing garments and shoes for factories, laundry or preparation of snacks to sell in the streets.

This was always in addition to their unpaid work at home which included cooking, cleaning, childcare, growing fruit and vegetables and keeping small animals. In 1897 one of the principal women's industries in the City of Peterborough was the picking of dried peas and sorting these by hand, removing the black or defective peas from the lighter. The rate of pay was said to be so small that even sixteen hours of work did not earn more than the day's subsistence.

The domestic servant was the single largest employer of women during the period this book covers, with 40 per cent of women in the provincial cities being employed in this way during the census of 1851 and 28 per cent (1.35 million) in 1911. The textiles/clothing sectors come a close second. Women provided a flexible, cheap and adaptive workforce for factories and sweat shops. With women earning a wage, their increasing independence and fashion consciousness meant that there was an increase in consumption of clothing, foodstuffs and home accessories.

Outside of the working classes some middle class women were involved in business and enterprise but this was generally frowned upon due to the Victorian ideals of motherhood and domestic orderliness. The legal status of married women and their limited property rights meant it was difficult for them to run a business on their own account until the 1880s. Widows often carried on the family business after the death of their husband. Spinsters often worked as governesses or in the millinery, inn-keeping, grocery, retail and other victualling trades.

In the First World War, large numbers of women were recruited into jobs that had been vacated by men who had gone to fight in the war. New jobs were also created as part of the war effort, for example, in munitions factories, for which Peterborough had a role. This high demand for weapons resulted in the munition factories becoming the largest single employer of women during 1918 – a social revolution for women which some say led to certain women being given the right to vote in that year. However, post war, many returning servicemen reclaimed their old jobs and the numbers of women workers declined heavily. During the 1920s and 1930s, the UK plunged into a recession which led to high levels of unemployment for both men and women. Although unemployment benefit had been introduced through the National Insurance Act of 1911, women were not eligible if they refused to take jobs in the domestic service sector and the benefit itself was much lower for women than men. However, in 1919, the Sex Disqualification Act made it easier for women to go to university and take up professional jobs as teachers or go into the civil service. By the 1930s one third of women over the age of 15 worked outside the home but one third still worked in domestic service but only one in ten married women worked. The new professions that were open to women had a marriage bar which meant that women had to resign from their posts when they got married.

The Second World War was a repeat of the First World War, where men went to fight and women took on their roles, despite, once more, concerns about women taking on men's work. In December 1941 women aged 20-30 were conscripted as auxiliaries to the Armed Forces, Civil Defence or in war industries. Post Second World War, the welfare state created many job opportunities in what was seen as women's work, particularly in the newly formed NHS.

On 30 November 1872, *The Peterborough and Huntingdon Standard* printed an article about the short stay of servant girls in situations and how much it inconvenienced mistresses and their households. The newspaper commented that its readers 'were not to be surprised to learn that girls would become unsettled in their situations when they saw the promises that were now held out to them', these notes offered bribes of some sort to encourage servants to change their posts. *The Standard* printed a note addressed to domestics which had been delivered to a lady's house near Peterborough from a Registry Office on All Saints Street in Stamford. Registry offices were the nineteenth century version of a modern-day employment agency. The note read:

> I take the liberty to inform you that if you required a situation as general servant or cook, I am in want of several immediately, and will obtain one for you if you will call, or forward by post my fee, which is 14 stamps.

The *Standard* hoped that when missives of this description were received by servants they would, as in this case, hand them promptly to their mistress. Of course, they may not do that.

Many advertisements in the newspapers stressed the need for the applications to be 'strong' or 'active' maids, particularly those from the country who were seen as healthier and more used to hard work in comparison to their urban counterparts. In the Post Office Directory for 1869, two registry offices were recorded in Peterborough.

In the 1861 census report for Northamptonshire there were 9,071 female and 763 male indoor servants, by 1881 female servants had increased to 11,076 and in 1901 stayed around the same at 11,022. The vast majority of these workers were engaged in small households as maids of all work.

****

In 1899 a lady called Matilda Hill (the wife of John Cathles Hill) set up an unusual partnership with John William Rowe. This was an extremely rare opportunity for a woman at this time. Mrs. Hill gave Mr. Rowe a large portion of the money he needed to purchase a plot of land for the brickworks of Dogsthorpe level crossing (named Dogsthorpe II). From 1899 onwards the duo traded as the Star Pressed Brick Co, and completed several local orders for important companies such as the Baker Perkins factories 1904–7, Peter Brotherhood's factory 1906–7 and the factory of Frederick Sage & Co. 1911. In 1904, Mr. Rowe and Mrs. Hill went on to buy a second site, nineteen acres of land at Kings Dyke, Whittlesey

****

At the start of the First World War, the harvest season came into full swing as recruitment into the army was increasing rapidly; there was a labour shortage and before long it became apparent that female workers would need to be found to toil in the fields and to milk the cows. The weather in August 1914 was fine and it was hoped it would continue so that the crops, which were at above average condition, could be gathered in the first fortnight – providing labour could be obtained.

At a special meeting of the Huntingdonshire County Council, which was presided over by the Earl of Sandwich, the chairman read out a letter from the local government board regarding the remuneration of women workers. This discussed the opinion that statistics were showing that Huntingdonshire women were not taking the place of men as they might, some women were taking part in ploughing or felling timber, but the majority were employed either in shops or at home and it was suggested that in the absence of the men, women might be employed with advantage much more than in the past.

The Symington corset factory was first founded by James Symington. He had married a Sarah Gold in 1835 who was experienced at stay making, a trade and craft essential for making corsets which, during this early period, were hand made and intricately embroidered. James himself owned a tailor and drapers shop. Their sons, Robert and William, saw the promise in Singer sewing machines and in 1856 they opened one of the first mechanised corset factories in England at Market Harborough, approximately 30 miles away from Peterborough.

By taking advantage of the drive of Victorian industrialisation, they turned the corset business into a huge success and before long were selling corsets across the globe. They soon expanded by opening other factories with their youngest daughter, Perry Gold Symington, who joined as a supervisor and executive – an unusual position for a woman at that time. The Peterborough site was opened in Bread Street (now known as Baker's Lane) in New Fletton in 1903, housing 250 machines. The factory measured approximately 46 x 32 metres and cost £6,000 to build. The City Council offered an incentive to the factory owners, a deal on electricity from the corporation works at a reduced cost of 2½d (approximately 81p today) per unit of electricity. The 1911 publication *Peterborough in Coronation Year* stated that the Symington factory was 'one of the leading factories of the Midlands with a worldwide trade', and which produced 'an article of universal wear – so universal that it ranks as a necessity'; the publication went on to say that the 300 girls in employment were producing '1,500 dozens per week which is a grand total of 18,000 garments a week'. In 1912, the premises were extended to house 450 machines, thus becoming highly labour-intensive, and for a time was the largest employer of females in Peterborough. The factory was further expanded in 1921 when the Peterborough branch replaced existing Symington factories in Desborough and Rothwell. At the time of the Second World War, Symington's in Peterborough employed around 650 workers (by 1956, a quarter of the staff had been employed for between thirty and forty years). For the duration of the war, the factory set aside the production of ladies corsets and undergarments and turned to war work. Still a major employer of women in Peterborough, it began producing parachutes, tropical shirts and gym shorts. Those families who had been involved in the factory's war effort were offered some parachute silk as a reward so that they could make extra clothing for themselves and eke out their clothing rations further, although some folk were not too happy with the colours available!

In the 1950s the factory reverted back into a Symington stitching station. A few accidents occurred on site; one worker, who joined Symington's in the 1950s straight after leaving school, recalled another girl working on her right suddenly going quiet, and saw that the co-worker had the sewing needle right through the middle of her finger. The machine wheel had to be turned round to release the victim's finger before any more damage was done and then help was sought. In 1967 the business was taken over by Courtaulds and many Symington factory branches closed, with the Peterborough factory soon being demolished. The only legacy to Symington now in Peterborough is the street name, Symington Close, in Woodston.

Another major factory in Peterborough was the Farrow canning factory, run by Joseph Farrow & Co. Ltd. Expanding sales saw their production factory relocated to a model factory at Fletton, Peterborough in 1902 from Boston in Lincolnshire, now not far from the notorious mustard fields in Wisbech. Allied to agricultural concerns, Farrows made canned foods – mainly green peas and then later marrowfat peas – at their Carlton Works in Fletton. In 1906 the company applied for patent labels for horseradish cream, Worcestershire sauce, mushroom ketchup, Farrows A1 mustard and A1 green peas. The canning factory was well known for exporting canned peas and fruit around the world. The workers at the factory were well looked after and great attention was paid to their health. No room was less than 12 foot high and there were a total of 335 windows within the six storey high building that also came with an octagonal shaft, it was a very imposing building. The Carlton Works were greatly extended in 1932. As a subsidiary of Reckitt & Colman the company also produced mushroom ketchup and mustard. Farrow's was also a major employer who provided work to a large number of women, particularly in the early summer when between 200 and 250 women and girls were employed to pick fruit as well as working with the processed peas.

Workers from Farrows were known to rent the nearby Hill houses, men were attracted to the Fletton area as with the development of these diverse industries, employment was easy to obtain and their wives and daughters could also find local work therefore retaining families in the area. Another key to the industry's success was the accessibility to the close-by railways. In fact, the percentage of female migrants arriving in Fletton was greater than the males. Ravenstein made observations about both Fletton and Huntingdonshire and noted that the 'woman is a greater migrant than man' in Fletton as employment was available at Farrow's Canning Factory, Symington's Corset Factory and domestic service locally, although there was competition for the non-domestic service positions as these offered better working conditions. There was an increasing percentage of females employed in dress and provision of food and lodging, and these employments were particularly attractive to unmarried female migrants. In comparison, half of the male migrant population were working on the railways or in the brickyards.

Advertisements began to appear in the *Peterborough Advertiser*, like this example from 15 October 1902, which enabled married women to work alongside their usual household chores:

Pea Pickers, Messrs. Farrow and Co. can supply peas to pick at pickers homes. Apply at the Mill, Fletton.

Pea Pickers wanted at the Mill. Farrow and Co. Fletton

John Cathles Hill was born in 1858 in Dundee, Forfarshire (Angus) and became known as the 'Maker of modern Fletton'. In the 1890s. Hill developed Harringay and Crouch End in North London using a steady supply of bricks at a good price from The London Brick Company in Fletton. Fletton then became his second home and as such he became increasingly conscious of the accommodation that his workers were living in. He thus built modern housing, put in new roads, made contributions towards new schools, erected shops, improved drainage and established local amenities such as The Coffee Palace which was a gentleman's club. The women and children were rewarded too, as his entire workforce, including the families were taken on day trips to Great Yarmouth and the food and entertainment was all paid for. Hill was paternalistic by nature and referred to as 'a just and generous employer'.

Fletton was an attractive place to live as it provided both secure employment and housing. In 1909 the London Brick Company had 340 houses on its rent roll in Fletton and Woodston, and in 1901 the rent for a house was between 3 and 4 shillings per week. Seasonal employment for women included assisting in the brickyards or they could secure employment at the nearby Symingtons in New Fletton, Farrows in Old Fletton or Cadge and Colemans by the East station. In Tebb's book *Peterborough,* Colemans was noted as being an 'enlightened' employer and was one of the first to offer holiday and sick pay to employees.

Some families who lived in Old Fletton, or moved into New Fletton, took in boarders to help make ends meet. 15.6 per cent of Fletton households had someone boarding with them – typically a male who had migrated to the area for work – a number of these, once they had settled at a job, moved into a local property and moved their family into the area. Many women became experienced lodging housekeepers, often running large establishments; widows and female heads of households looking for a way to boost their income could offer boarding and reduce housing shortages. The Bakehouse in Fletton was the place where communal baking took place giving wives a chance to get together to forge friendships and share news.

Between 1841 and 1911 Fletton transformed from a rural village with a population of 246 into a community of 4,742. New Fletton was the developing railway community with predominately privately owned and rented housing and Old Fletton was the brick workers community with housing built by Hill. These communities were split by Fletton Spring.

Hill's houses, set along tree lined roads, were identical in each having a small front garden and a long rear garden for vegetable growing and pig keeping. In 1897 electric lighting was installed, with the electric lights consisting of 3 arc lights of 1,500 candles each, and 30 incandescent lights of 30 candles which allowed for night time working. However, the residents of Old Fletton found them 'so dazzling that the roadway could not be seen' and a request was made by the Norman Cross Rural District Council that a shade should be fitted to 'prevent the glaring light'. There was also complaints that the sewage from the housing developments was running straight into the brook in Love Lane, Old Fletton, there were concerns that there might be an outbreak or an epidemic due to this drainage system.

Pantiles Housing Society came up with a scheme in 1928 to build three blocks of flats for bachelor lady tenants. The plan was to have twelve flats in the three blocks, set in a courtyard facing All Saints Church on Park Road. Within the centre of the courtyard would be a permanently-on electric light so that each block entrance would be well lit. An artist's impression of one of the blocks was printed in the *Peterborough and Huntingdonshire Standard* on 27 February, however it seems that the scheme never came to fruition.

Milton Hall was the largest private house in the area and was the historical home of the Fitzwilliam family. During both World Wars the house was lent out to the military, with the family instead living in Longthorpe House. In 1917, when the hall housed an auxiliary hospital/convalescence home, the rooms, such as the Pillared Hall, Smoking Room, Long Gallery and the Peterborough Rooms, were all filled with rows of iron beds while the Old Masters remained on the walls.

In nearby Castor quite a few women were listed in the 1874 Trade Directory as having their own business, with six female farmers out of twenty-four, such as Ann Dickens at Top Lodge Farm in Upton, and other roles such as a coal merchant, a grocer and baker, two shoemakers, a butcher, a shopkeeper and baker, and another shopkeeper.

Female workers were also employed at the Peter Brotherhood headquarters at Walton. During 1927 a number of large turbines were being built by Brotherhood for a nearby power station. Peter Brotherhood had been at its current location since 1907 thanks to the good land and railway connections. During the First World War the company employed over 2,000 staff. These workers were employed to produce munitions, tank engines, torpedo parts and items relating to battleships. Werner Pfeiderer & Perkins, who changed their name to Perkins Engineers due to the German connotations, also produced munitions during the war thus employing female workers, as well as Frederick Sage & Co in Walton who made seaplanes for the navy and Westwood Works was notable for the number of women working on machine tools.

Women munition workers from Werner Pfleiderer & Perkins Ltd were seen parading through Peterborough Market Place on 14 September 1918, just prior to the end of the First World War. The *Peterborough Advertiser* states 'Between 500 and 600 Women War Workers in their picturesque uniforms attended a Women's Recruiting Rally at Peterborough on Saturday. There were the WAC and WRNS and WRAF, the VADs, munition workers, and others in their uniforms or overalls. The munition workers brought up the rear guard of the parade and were praised for the work they did, not having the advantages of working in the open air.'

Women's Land Army in Peterborough. Recruitment numbers

Year	Number of Girls Registered
1917	532
1918	514
1919	575
1920	814
1921	816
1922	575
1923	514

The Peterborough Celta Mill strike in 1928

In December 1928, eighteen people appeared at the Norman Cross Petty Sessions in Peterborough for 'breach of contract' and 'wrongful absence from work' from the Celta artificial silk mill, which was owned by Messrs. Kemil Ltd. The Peterborough Trades Union Council (PTUC) have suggested that the industrial action at the Celta Mill in 1928 had resulted in the longest strike action in Peterborough's industrial history. Many women were involved in the strike, which was unusual for the time.

The mill opened in 1924 during the inter-war period in a period of economic uncertainty and mass unemployment. The arrival of the mill was important to the local economy because it provided plenty of new jobs in the area. Artificial silk was made from Canadian Fir using the viscose process, however this involved the use of dangerous chemicals such as caustic soda. The mill ran continuously, using three work shifts a day. The strike started on Thursday, 25 October, the day after a spinner was suspended for allowing viscose to drip into a 7lb tin of prepared artificial silk. The Thursday afternoon shift did not turn up to work and by Friday there were 1,000 people out on a strike with most belonging to the Workers Union. Women occupied 1,500 of the 2,000 positions that had been created at the mill. As a result, the Worker's Union's women's organisers from Birmingham and London, Miss Weaver and Kate Manicom, came to Peterborough and spoke at the strike rallies, as well as Clara Rackham, the campaigner for social justice and prospective Labour parliamentary candidate for Huntingdonshire, who attended a meeting to explain the reasoning behind the dispute to the parents of striking girls. Clara Rackham was a factory inspector during the First World War and was knowledgeable about factory conditions. Although women were involved in the strike, only the male workers were summoned to the court – the men were charged a small amount for the damages (1 shillings), and 2 shillings and six pence costs. The mill's manager, Claude Isch-Wall, took the men concerned for beer and cigarettes at a nearby hotel afterwards. Business declined rapidly after the strikes, 300 members of staff were laid off in the early 1930s and the mill shut down shortly afterwards.

The diary of a 25-year-old chambermaid who worked at the Great Northern Hotel in Peterborough in 1935 describes how her normal working day started at 6 am and ended at 10 pm, with two hours off in between. Unmarried staff lived in the hotel, and women were accommodated above the kitchen as it was warm during the winter. Chambermaids bought their own uniforms, which consisted of a blue dress for the mornings and a black one for the afternoons. They earned 10 shillings per week, including accommodation and meals, and the staff had the pick of whatever was left on the menu. In the late 1930s, the bathrooms were the only rooms that had radiators, so the building was freezing cold during the winter. Laura worked at the hotel until it closed down due to the outbreak of the Second World War in 1939. The hotel itself reopened in 1949 after extensive repairs and in the 1950s was a popular wedding reception and is still open today.

From Spring 1941, every woman in Britain, aged between 18 and 60, had to be recorded and their family's occupations listed. Each was interviewed, and required to select from a list of jobs, although it was made clear that women were not required to bear arms. It is said that on 19 April 1941, around 800 20-year-old girls answered their call up papers with some girls coming with their mothers, some with boyfriends and others with their perambulators, which they left lined up outside the recruitment office! Choices included the WVS (the Women's Voluntary Service, the largest women's organisation), the ATS (Auxiliary Territorial Service, formed in 1938), the WAAF (the Women's Auxiliary Air Force) and the Women's Land Army.

By Saturday 14 June 1941, 514 women (minus a few late entries) born in 1918 had registered for national duty at the Peterborough Employment Exchange for work of national importance. It is thought that the reason for the fall in numbers for the 1918 category is that births may have been fewer in the last few years of the First World War compared to the two following it due to the men having been involved in the war and away from their wives. There were no female conscientious objectors.

A high percentage of those who signed up from previous age groups, such as those who were born in 1921, were already on war work. There was an announcement printed in the *Standard* on Friday 13 June 1941, stating that the town clerk had been authorised to take proceedings against people who failed to register for civil defence duties and this had a salutary effect.

In October 1941, it was announced that all women between the ages of 20 and 25 who worked in the retail trade (other than food) were to be considered for recruitment to the women's auxiliary services or other vital war work. Unfortunately, this instruction would cause some significant inconvenience to local traders. With trade already slowing down, they would lose their trained staff and would have to rely on the younger and inexperienced. A lot of shop girls had already put themselves forwards for munitions work to avoid being sent out of town on war duty, and with the 20–25 category disappearing, shops would now be extremely short staffed. Large stores such as Marks and Spencer and Woolworth lost 50–55 per cent of their staff and some departments, and even establishments, were forced to close down. However, Mr. Compton, the Drapery Manager at the Co-operative Society made an important statement: 'If it is essential, the girls must go, for winning the war is the most important job before us, if we don't win the war, it will be no use opening at all.' Some thought it was unfair that the retail trade had to bear the brunt of the loss of staff while others such as the Post Office, the Town Hall and government offices kept theirs.

During the Second World War, the Post Office was the single largest employer in women. Historically, the Post Office had discriminated against women, but as the Armed Forces requested that the Post Office should release staff for war purposes, women became increasingly important to the organisation. Management began to actively recruit and train women for the skilled tasks formerly performed by men. On 9 January 1942, 334 female candidates applied for training as postal engineers. Out of these, 36 were to be trained at a special school in Peterborough. Over 100 were needed in the district but lack of opportunity to train these ladies was holding up any possible recruitment. Just before the war started, the Post Office experienced an expansion of operations, such as in the field of telegraphy, and it was felt by both the Government and the Post Office that public communication services needed improving, particularly because these had proved insufficient in the previous war. More and more trunk calls were being made, which needed an operator to connect and, as such, the Post Office increased its staff by 5,000 employees in 1930-5, with a further 5,000 women recruited in 1935.

On 28 October there were 547 registrations of women born in 1914 at the Employment Exchange. All interviews of the women in their various age groups were going well, it was reported, and they all had a 'helpful attitude'. A number of women were making applications for the ATS (Auxiliary Territorial Service) and other similar services. The biggest problem with recruitment was due to some employers being reluctant to take on women workers, believing that they were incapable of carrying out work usually done by men;

when it was pointed out that the welfare of the country depended on these women, however, employers usually changed their minds. Two ladies had been employed in road work, weeding and carrying out general cleaning of the roads and footpaths. They had been employed through the Exchange centre and were paid 10d. an hour. The National Service Conscription for Women Act came into force on the 18 December 1941.

On 7 March 1942, 619 women aged 35 were registered at the Peterborough Employment Exchange and a large percentage of these ladies registered their occupation as domestic responsibilities.

It was the turn of the 16-year-olds to register on Saturday, 25 April 1942, these numbered 712. Any girls who were not attached to any youth organisation would be interviewed with a view to finding an organisation or interest for them to join, such as the St John Ambulance Brigade, canteen work, gardening, or some sort of pre-service training for the ATS, WAAFS or WRNS.

A state registration order was made for nurses and midwives on 10 April 1943. Many more than was expected turned up at the Peterborough Employment Exchange and so they didn't have enough forms ready for the approximately 400 who registered; 232 were employed in nursing or midwifery or had practised in the previous twelve months, and 158 had nursing experience but had not practised recently. Already working at the Memorial Hospital was a matron and staff of sixty-four, of which seventeen were sisters and forty-six nurses. This would bring the total of nurses and midwives to well over 450 and this was without any postal registrations. It was reported that these women seemed eager to register and although most wished to remain in Peterborough, quite a few women stated that they did not mind where they were posted to.

The shortage of labour on farms was becoming an issue once more in the Peterborough area. A meeting of the Executive Committee of the Peterborough County Branch of the NFU on 6 October 1943 discussed how men were unavailable, and that women were now heavily involved in munitions and alternative war work in comparison to other years. The committee decided to employ instead boys aged 14 to 19, however, eight weeks would be needed to train these boys.

Horsey Toll is situated just outside Stanground and within close proximity to RAF Westwood. The site during the Second World War had searchlights and anti-aircraft guns to protect the Civilian Repair Depot (CRD) located at a private landing field at Shortacres Farm 2.5 miles east of Peterborough which belonged to Mr. Hugh Abinger Whittome and later, his son Kenneth Whittome. The airfield itself became licensed in May 1930, but was closed at the start of the Second World War; in 1940, Lord Beaverbrook, the Minister of Aircraft Production, established an organisation where a number of institutions were seconded to overhaul and repair damaged Hurricanes and parts of Wellingtons. The Civilian Repair Organisation (CRO) would also repair and overhaul other battle-damaged aircraft which, once fixed, would be sent on to training units or other air forces. These CROs would employ women in this important war work.

One of the companies seconded by the Civilian Repair Organisation was Morrisons Engineering Ltd based in Croydon. Morrisons were aeronautical and general engineers who specialised in aircraft assemblies, welding and heat-treatment. During the Second World War, Morrisons Engineering purchased Horsey Toll airfield and converted the aircraft hangers into factory units where cotton fabric was used on aircraft wings and then doped (a type of plastic lacquer used to reinforce the airframes and make them waterproof and airtight). Typical doping agents were nitro cellulose, cellulose acetate and cellulose acetate bullyrate; the liquid dopes could be highly flammable. A number of women worked in the Civilian Repair Unit at Horsey Toll assisting with repairing severely damaged aircraft such as broken fuselages, ailerons and air frames. During July 1940 Horsey was returning 150 repaired aircraft a week, and by December 1940 the CRD had seen 4,995 aircraft pass through the factory. This little known factory made a massive contribution to the war effort and the ladies who worked there earned wing badges for their assistance.

American servicewomen were honoured for their work in the local area by a special luncheon in the reception room of Peterborough Town Hall which was hosted by the mayor, Mr. Harry Kelley JP, and Mary, the Princess Royal and Countess of Harewood, also attended. Prior to the luncheon, a group of American nurses were given a tour of Peterborough Cathedral by the Dean and were shown where Mary, Queen of Scots was buried before her son James I, transferred her to Westminster Abbey.

CHAPTER FOUR

Home life in Peterborough

Fashion

One of the highlights for women shopping for new clothing items was the advertisements in local newspapers, such as the below, whereby new fashion pieces were brought to Peterborough. In the *Peterborough Advertiser* on 29 September 1855, Miss Brown announced that she had recently returned from London with 'all the latest Novelties from Paris, in Embroidery, Collarets, Sleeves, Bugle and other Head-dresses with the Eugenia Falls and Barbs'. The items would be available for viewing on Tuesday 2 October and during the next Fair. An advertisement in the *Peterborough Standard*, 6 April 1870, carried an advertisement for Mrs. and Miss Simms, who were begging 'to invite the Ladies of Peterborough to their show of Millinery of the greatest variety'. The establishment at No.2, Cobden Terrace, Cemetery Road, Peterborough, sold bonnets of the latest designs straight from London ready for the new season, mantles, evening and other dresses in new styles as well as other fancy articles that were sure to please. The advertisement also gratefully thanked the ladies of Peterborough for their previous custom and hoped for their continued support. Fashion advice was printed in the local newspapers such as in the *Peterborough Advertiser*, 21 November 1897 – 'FASHION IN SLEEVES: we learn from Myra's Journal (of dress and fashion) that the Spring sleeves promise to be very pretty. The new sleeves are tight, with a slight fullness or a small drapery at the shoulder. The best dressmakers try as much as possible to cut drapery and sleeve together, as the effect is always better. Ruffled sleeves remain fashionable, and tucked sleeve is daily becoming more prevalent.'

Food

Food related advertisements could often be found in the *Peterborough Advertiser* such as: 'BREAD! BREAD!! BREAD!!! – Is regularly supplied to Families in any part of the city by J. ELLABY, Albert Place, Peterbro: warranted free from Rice, Alum, or Potatoes.' or 'CHEAP FOOD FOR PIGS. A LARGE Consignment of GROUND RICE for feeding Pigs, in bags containing 14 stones, at 16s 6d per bag, bag included' were printed in the September issue of the newspaper.

The women of Peterborough could frequently be found shopping in the market in the city centre. Since the Market Charter was granted in 1143, the market in Peterborough has taken place on a Wednesday, opposite the Greyhound public house, on the Market Square (formerly Cathedral Square), run by farmers and butchers. In 1863 the market was so popular that the Peterborough Cattle Market Company was formed and a site was bought from Earl Fitzwilliam, with the new market being opened in 1865. At the time it was twice the size of the current market site and included the Embassy Theatre. The new market was well timed because, with the coming of the railway, Peterborough had developed a large wholesale butchery contract with Smithfields in London. By the end of the nineteenth century a couple of rows of stalls had appeared across the square directly opposite the Minster Gate and these sold fruit and market-garden produce. Nearby were auctioneer squares, and pitches for quack doctors, herbalists and wandering cheapjacks (hawkers or peddlers). The auctioneers sold a wide range of second-hand furniture and odds and ends. This became the focal point for crowds of people mid-week.

There was also a fish market in Church Street, but this generated many complaints from those who went to church on a Sunday and could still smell Saturday's fish! The fried-fish stall on a Wednesday also drew adverse comments, however the Town Clerk told the Royal Commission on Market Fairs and Tolls that these complaints were not serious enough 'to warrant the council providing ... a covered market ... at public expense'.

The Corporation laid out a chartered Saturday market and supplied the stalls. These were usually occupied by local traders or market gardeners from the local area and as such were grouped together by trade. For example, the butchers held the front four rows and attended regularly, with some stalls remaining in the same family for generations. The butter-market was run under the Guildhall, and Fen women had been selling poultry, eggs, and butter there for centuries. In 1901 it was reported that 'Mr. Bristow, the Head Constable, two or three times a year, had the Butter Cross Gates locked and all the butter weighed. All that underweight was taken away, and, I believe, given to the poor.'

The Town Clerk also reported in 1888 of the Butter market: 'Hobbes, the beadle, used to consider that the chairs on which people sit and that he had the exclusive rights of charging a penny for each chair used. The man is now dead and the Corporation have purchased the chairs for what they are worth.' The Guildhall was renovated in 1927, the butter gates taken away and the last butter woman, Mrs Bellairs, was given a stall on the general market.

The 1888 tolls for a market stall were 6*d* for a 10ft stall with no awning and 1*s* 6*d* for a butcher's stall with a frame that could take a canvas cover. The butchers toll included a fee of 6*d* because the Council scrubbed the butcher's boards between markets. Moving forward to 1914, the tolls were not much different, a low stall cost 1*d* per ft, and those which were in the prime positions on the edges of the square were 2*s* 3*d* and the others 2*s*. By 1950, at the end of the period covered in this book, the prices for the best positioned stalls were 22*s* 6*d*. In 1925 the City Council decided to add electric lighting to the market and it was compulsory to have at least one 60 watt bulb for each stall. The city supplied all of the fittings and bulbs at 1*s* a light a day. Extra lights were provided at the stall holder's request. After this period, auctioneers decreased in number, and quack doctors and cheapjacks were banned with the number of stallholders beginning to increase.

Weddings

Before the motoring age, the Angel Hotel, formerly of 47 Narrow Bridge Street was rumoured to be the best wedding turn out and many girls booked their horse and trap from here. The Hotel was an inn for over 500 years, at first belonging to the Abbey and then becoming an important coaching inn before being demolished in 1972. In 1881 it was run by John Core, an Alderman of the Corporation and hotel keeper along with his wife, 7 female servants and 3 male servants. The main room was available to be booked for concerts, balls, wedding breakfasts, dinners and public entertainments. In the 1930s the Angel became the city's first AA/RAC three star hotel and then later during the Second World War it was the base for the city's volunteer fire department.

Transport

The arrival of the railways turned Peterborough rapidly into a boom town. A number of developments started popping up which were to change the character of the city forever, particularly as the population was rapidly growing. The new marshalling yards and other railway installations were very labour intensive and, as such, housing for the railway workers was in huge demand. New homes for the railway workers and their families sprang up in the area between the North Station and almost to Walton. The Great Northern line actually set up a whole new community for their staff consisting of pubs, churches, schools, shops and, of course, homes. The men who took up residence here were mainly employed in the marshalling yards and engine yards. Numbers 620-736 Lincoln Road are all that remain of the 227 houses, known as the Barracks, that were built by the Great Northern Railway (GNR). This development was of such a standard that by general approval the name of New England was given. The accommodation provided was superior for the period and included gas, supplied by the company's own gasworks as well as water and drains. The GNR also funded 80 per cent of the nearby St Paul's Parish Church. Other encampments of railway workers housing could be found locally: Midland Railway employees were based at Spital Bridge, London and North Western Railway employees were to be found at Woodston, and the Great Eastern Railway workers in Fletton. At the end of the nineteenth century, over 25 per cent of the working population of Peterborough could be found working on the railways. Rows of decorated Victorian red bricked houses remain against a background of the echo of trains.

Peterborough East opened on 2 June 1845 at the end of a 47 mile branch line from the London & Birmingham Railway via Northampton, Thrapston, Oundle and Wansford (a portion survives today as part of the Nene Valley Railway). The present mainline station was opened by the Great Northern Railway on 7 August 1850, names suggested for the new station included: Cowgate, Priestgate and Peterborough. Rails services peaked in 1910 but economies were made during the First World War and the railways never recovered. The East station closed in 1966.

In addition to the railway, Peterborough was also served by a tram network; electric tramways had taken over from horse buses from 24 January 1903 and subsequently operated within Peterborough for a further twenty-seven years, until 15 November 1930.

There were three routes in the infrastructure:

- Running along Westgate and Lincoln Road to a terminus at the junction with Sage's Lane.
- Running along Westgate, Lincoln road and Dogsthorpe Road to a terminus at the junction with St Paul's Road.
- Running along Midgate, New Road and Eastfield Road to a terminus at the junction with Eye Road.

The Car 10's tram terminus, run by the Peterborough District Tram Company, was situated in Walton Road (now part of Lincoln Road) and in 1906, a Mrs. Johnston was well known for selling tea and a bun for $1d$ from her home on the same street. Her house was also used as the collection depot for any parcels delivered by tram. Recreationally trams would be taken to Walton and then local citizens could walk either to Werrington or Marholm Woods. The fleet of 14 British Brush Electrical Machines open top double deck tramcars initially had a livery of lake brown and cream, which was later changed to holly and cream.

Like other tram systems across the country, the Peterborough District Tram Company employed women during the Great War, generally as conductresses but a few years later, also as motor women to replace the men who had been called up into the armed forces. Uniforms would have been long skirts with long-double breasted coats with two rows of five buttons, lapels and epaulettes. A wide-trimmed waterproof bonnet would have been worn which would have carried the standard British Electric Traction Company magnet and wheel cap badge on the band. In comparison to other tramways companies who released women staff when the men returned from the war, the Peterborough District Tram Company continued to employ female staff until the closure of the system in 1930.

Lighting

On 31 March 1900 Peterborough got electric street lighting after twenty-one years of procrastination, thanks to competition between gas and electric lighting, as well as the requirement of a £20,000 loan to finance the project, which was finally sanctioned in 1898. A concert in aid of raising money for the Fund for Lighting the Streets was held 26 February 1889 by the Yaxley Glee Class in the girls' schoolroom as described in the Yaxley Deanery Magazine. The majority of the performers were residents in the local parish and were described as being very talented, with many encores demanded. Around £4 was raised for the fund after paying expenses.

On 9 January 1915 the order for all external lights to be shaded came into force in Peterborough for fear of German air raids. This made the streets very quiet and sombre at night.

Floods

During 1848, while the Bridge Fair was held, a boat could be seen sailing down Bridge Street to the Golden Lion and similar recorded floods occurred again in 1912 and 1916, when there was extensive widespread flooding following three weeks of heavy rainfall at the end of August. On 26 August 1912 there was 13½ hours of rain between 5.30 am and 7 pm; by 8 pm on the following day, 27 August, the River Nene had risen to 17ft 6in. In areas like Bodger's Yard, planks or ladders had to be erected as a temporary walkway to enable residents to enter or exit their homes from their bedroom windows, with many places they could only access via the upper floor. The city centre streets were awash with flood water and people living in the affected area not only had to move their furniture and belongings upstairs but also their pigs and other livestock. *The Sphere: An Illustrated Newspaper for the Home* dated 7 September 1912 had a front page picture depicting a half-submerged parlour and a lady trying to scoop water out with a saucepan. The floods at the town bridge drew large crowds as the water levels reached 7ft above their normal levels and many people crowded onto the bridge to look, causing huge safety concerns at the time.

CHAPTER FIVE

Women and the Wars

Right at the start of the First World War the mayor of Peterborough made a civic appeal in regards to food frugality:

> In my capacity as your mayor I venture to address a few words to you at this critical juncture in our national affairs. Our country will probably be actively involved in the greatest European conflagration since the days of Napoleon. Ample food supplies are assured. Not only have we four months supply already in the country, but today in the House of Commons a Government scheme has been propounded for the national insurance of all British ships carrying food and raw material to our shores so that if people act wisely AND ONLY PURCHASE FOR THEIR DAILY NEEDS, prices will be kept within reasonable limits and our trade and manufacturers will proceed as usual. The Government are also taking steps to set up a national scheme of help for those who may, through unemployment or other adverse circumstances, be short of the necessities of life. [...] It behoves us all therefore to conduct ourselves with calmness and discretion and above all, to avoid any action which might result in causing panic or increasing distress. Also in our homes to be careful with regard to food – THAT THERE SHOULD BE NO WASTE – and whatever our position may be we should live FRUGALLY and SOBERLY for the coming weeks, or it may be months, and so economise in this and other ways in the interest of our poorer fellow citizens.

On 9 January 1915 the order for all external lights to be shaded came into force in Peterborough for fear of German air raids. This made the streets very quiet and sombre at night.

Many of the men who signed up to the Great War left in Pals battalions; this meant that brothers and friends left together, fought together, and frequently died together. This greatly affected the families left behind in Peterborough. Well over 1,000 men lost their lives and are recorded in the First World War Memorial book which was unveiled in Peterborough Cathedral on 11 November 2007.

Ethel Banister was the only female casualty of the Great War, the third daughter of Mr. and Mrs. T. Banister who resided in the Greyhound Public House in Market Place. Ethel was travelling on the RMS *Hesperian* from Liverpool to Quebec when it was hit by a torpedo from German U-boat SM *U-20* (the same one that sank the *Lusitania*) on the night of 4 September 1915 and subsequently sank while being towed to Ireland on 6 September. 32 passengers, 8 of which were female, including Ethel Banister, drowned when their lifeboat upset while lowering. Ethel had been making the trip to Vancouver in Canada to visit her married sister.

Although the Second World War had not yet been declared, construction had started on sixty-five air raid shelters to accommodate anyone who found themselves in the street during an air raid. There would be space for a total of 3,250 people across the city. Each individual shelter would be able to hold 50 people and was 43ft long, 7ft wide, and gave 6ft 4in of headroom. Inside would be three rows of benches and three lavatories, and the shelters would be open all day with an attendant. Although each shelter was designed to be splinter-proof and gas-proof, they would not withstand a direct hit; Peterborough was not deemed a vulnerable area by the authorities, despite the high number of factories and railways.

The locations for the air raid shelters would be as follows:

Bishop's Road Car Park	19 Shelters	950 people
New England Recreation Ground	7 shelters	350 people
Fletton Recreation Ground	7 shelters	350 people
Stanley Recreation Ground	22 shelters	1,100 people
Burghley Square (two sites)	7 shelters	350 people
Trinity Square Slipper Baths	3 shelters	150 people

Employers had to provide shelters for their employees, such as Joseph Farrow & Co's works and offices at Old Fletton. Farrow provided 3 reinforced underground shelters which were able to accommodate 400 to 500 workers, as well as an underground hospital, warning sirens and a firefighting system. Each of these shelters came with electric lighting, ventilation, telephones and lavatories. The occupants of these underground shelters were protected from direct blasts too. Two shelters were located near the railway bridge and the other directly on the works' premises.

Despite Peterborough having an RAF flying training aerodrome, a Royal Ordnance factory, a training centre for special forces at Milton Hall and many factories engaged in important wartime production, the city was still considered a safe destination for evacuees from London. By mid-September 1939 already 5,479 evacuees had been sent to the Soke of Peterborough. In October, some further evacuees from the Bentall Road Mixed School arrived through the Government's No.2 scheme and went to the Walton area. The first baby to be born to an evacuee mother also arrived in October and was born at the maternity ward in St John's Hospital. The mayor gave the newborn a souvenir spoon bearing the city's arms.

The following year, in October 1940, another 1,000 evacuees arrived from London causing further headache to Peterborough's officials as accommodation needed to be found for these incomers and mothers with large families were reluctant to be separated from their offspring. The number of evacuees now totalled 8,562, although some had gone back to London without telling the authorities. Schools, the Milk Office and the Food Control Department were under pressure to keep up with the new intakes as well as making billeting arrangements.

> Local authorities at the unspecified destination within the specified distance range – from Kent to Peterborough – were in charge of the billeting, that no attempt of private billet search should be made and that the government would pay the billeting cost.

By 1944, evacuees were still arriving in Peterborough and the surrounding area thanks to the Doodlebugs and V2 rockets targeting London and the South East. The billeting officials and the WVS were in charge of securing accommodation for both families and unaccompanied schoolchildren, but were finding it increasingly difficult to find billets and some had to be relocated to other parts of the country.

Statistics extracted from R.M. Titmuss' *Problems of Social Policy: History of the Second World War* suggested in the Soke of Peterborough, the number of evacuees received by September 1939 were 2,424, a mere 15 per cent received in comparison to numbers expected.

At the beginning of the Second World War pupils from Queens Head Street School in Islington, London, were evacuated to the country along with their teachers. They were taken by train to their destination, taken to a hall where local residents picked up their chosen child/ren and then each pupil sent a postcard home giving their new address in Peterborough. Some evacuee boys from the school were reported to have helped the farmers with the harvest and took part in fishing with makeshift rods at Eye. Mrs. Fox and her daughter took in 4 children to live with them at their shop in Castor Green. If you lived in the villages you were lucky if you had electricity or water. Buckets had to be carried from the nearest pump and toilets might be shared, and were generally at the bottom of the garden.

In March 1940, Eva Smith of 73 Broadway was brought before the Peterborough magistrates for allowing a light to shine from a side window of her house; on 3 February, PC Hubble spotted that the entirety of her garden, as well as a wall 30 ft away was lit up. Ms. Smith was fined £1 for committing a blackout regulation offence. Annie Quin of Scotney Street was also fined at the same court for using an unauthorised front lamp on her bicycle. In 1943, Dorothy Wood of Broadway Gardens, Peterborough was fined £2 for allowing a light to be unobscured at 9.45 pm on 15 April. Mrs. Wood said that her children must have got up and put the light on, which they admitted. The Chairman of the magistrates noted that the offence was committed not long after the blackout.

Christmas was a solemn affair during the Second World War; many of the local men were away in the forces and were sent many parcels by their loved ones. The mayor and mayoress spent their lunch time visiting the four hospitals – St John's, Thorpe Road House, the Memorial Hospital and the Isolation Hospital, before returning home to their family. Due to the war, Boxing Day in 1940 was cancelled so the only official holiday was on the big day itself and so everyone attempted to enjoy the spirit of festivities. The *Standard* organised a party a few days later for the children of men serving in the forces and catered for over 400 children aged between 5 and 14. Later in 1941, the Post Office had to hire extra workers to cope with the Christmas rush of extra post, with local women, men from local Artillery Regiments and senior children drafted in from the local schools to help. The Corn Exchange was used as an overflow depot and some five-ton lorries were used to transfer parcels to and from Peterborough North Station.

The National Registration Bill required a compilation of a National Register, so on 29 September 1939, registration was to take place in Peterborough with 101 enumerators covering the approximately 85,000 people living within the city and local district. Each enumerator had to make out each individual identity card with the parents being given their children's cards to look after. Identity cards were meant to be carried at all times, although a survey carried out by a *Standard* reporter found that only one in twenty were. However, by the end of 1944, citizens, including girls, were being fined by the magistrates courts for not being able to produce their identity cards when asked. Such as in the case of Ivy and Violet Ferris of St John's Street who were caught by the police who stopped an American lorry in which they were travelling. Both girls were given two days in which to produce their cards at a police station, but turned up late and found themselves summoned. Only Violet turned up at the magistrates, both girls were fined five shillings each. Women from Peterborough were frequently seen with the American soldiers who were stationed close by on the airbases.

Once a person had their identity card they were entitled to the new food rationing card/book. Later on 23 August, registration for milk had to be completed to ensure that each child and all pregnant mothers were able to receive one pint of milk a day, whereas the rest of the population was entitled to only half-a-pint a day. The largest milk distributor in Peterborough was the Co-operative Dairy on Midland Road. Rationing led to long queues developing in the centre of Peterborough with folk convinced that the shopkeepers were not going to share out the newly arrived wares fairly.

The clothing depot in Cowgate was run by the WVS and was stocked with consignments from the American Red Cross. Coupons had to be provided by the customer after applying to the Public Assistance organisation, but there was never a lack of stock for customers at the shop run by Mrs. Dickens and Mrs. Jordan. Should homes be bombed, there were a number of rest centres containing complete outfits of clothing for anyone in desperate need.

The first air raid that hit Peterborough by the Luftwaffe was on 8 June 1940 and it directly hit the Lido swimming pool (which was quickly restored post war). On 16 November 1940, the Fletton area took a pounding from bombs with 31 people injured. The 10 May 1941 saw the heaviest night of the bombing in Britain. Bombs too fell in Peterborough and two firefighters that night lost their lives. The bombs hit in the vicinity of the new museum, across Priestgate and into Cowgate. In Cross Street, after the all clear, firefighters went to investigate a badly damaged building to check if anyone was trapped inside and an unexploded incendiary device went off. 250 bombs were dropped on 10 August 1942, 6 of which hit the Cathedral roof. The Air Raid Protection volunteers helped effectively protect against extensive damage. The public air raid shelter in Priestgate Vaults underneath the museum building, within the cellars, is still intact and is now a display. The caretaker of the museum during the Second World War was a Mr. Winter who also lived in the building and was a volunteer with the Home Guard. An Edna Kingston died on 14 November 1941, following injuries received from the air raid of 10 May. Her father died some twelve days later, also due to injuries received from the same air raid. Their cottage had been demolished by a bomb that landed in Cross Street.

The museum is one of the city's most historic buildings. Originally it was a private house that dated from 1816 and was built for local magistrate Thomas Cooke. The cellars beneath the property date from an older sixteenth-century building. The mansion was sold in 1856 to Earl Fitzwilliam and it was then converted into a public dispensary and infirmary thus becoming the city's first hospital, employing a number of nurses, until the opening of the new War Memorial Hospital. Infectious cases were sent to a separate hospital at Fengate known as St Peter's, where diseases such as Diphtheria and Scarlet Fever were treated after the hospital opened in 1901 on the site of Low Farm. There was severe fire damage to the infirmary building at Priestgate in 1884 and in 1897 the first purpose built operating theatre was opened as an extension to the current hospital. The operating theatre offered state of the art care for the people of Peterborough and incorporated the most up to date medical ideas including the use of anesthesia and keeping the theatre meticulously clean. The funds that went towards building the operating theatre were anonymous donations from two Peterborough women who simply wished to be known as 'Heliotrope'. In 1931 the property was acquired by the Museum Society in 1931 and an art gallery was added in 1939. The museum is the most haunted location in the city of Peterborough.

Other hospitals could be found in Peterborough between 1850 and 1950. In the 1860's there was a Fever Hospital on Trinity Street which later became the Slipper Baths. A short-term smallpox hospital on Newark Common and at Eye in 1878. The Fengate smallpox hospital in 1936 was recorded in the Kelly's Northants Directory as having 38 beds and two staff at the institution. had a sewage farm within the grounds before it was demolished in 1978 and curiously buried under six foot of soil. Thorpe Lawn House was commandeered during the First World War for the rehabilitation of wounded men as well as Barnwell Castle, Milton Park and the Palace which were turned into Red Cross Auxiliary Hospitals. Peterborough's workhouse infirmary was replaced and renamed, in the 1920s, as St John's. In later years St John's took in maternity patients and then in 1947 changed clients to the mentally ill.

In April 1942, Mr. Baker, a secretary for the Committee for Imported Fruit Distribution, announced that supplies of oranges would be available in shops within the Peterborough area. The fruit would initially be reserved, for five days, for children who were in possession of a green ration book; they would be entitled to 1 lb. of oranges each. After the five days had elapsed, the oranges would be made available to everyone, however priority should be given to children, invalids and those in hospital.

New ration books were introduced in 1942, but by 28 May only 40,000 of the 75,000 replacement books had been issued. The *Standard* revealed that particular schools would be open the coming Saturday for the purpose which would offer a welcome alternative to queueing at the food office. Food rationing had increased by the time another set of rationing books were issued between 4–8 June 1945 from the Corn Exchange, with the Deputy Food Executive Officer, Mr. Frank Smith, also the City's Treasurer, overseeing the entire operation. Further distribution would be made from the Old Council Offices in Fletton and subsequently from the villages surrounding Peterborough city.

At Christmas 1943, there were large queues outside of Patens in Long Causeway as hundreds of men and women waited in line in order to be able to buy a quarter bottle of gin or whisky. Previously in 1941, there were shortages of fruit, spirits and wine, and anything that was available was sold at higher than usual prices. The Peterborough Co-op struggled to sell toys with only £700 worth sold in comparison to £2,000 the year before. The Peterborough

Advertiser reported on the Christmas poultry market of 1943 that it 'was remarkable for an almost total absence of birds' and it was said that there wasn't even a turkey available for the mayor's traditional visit to the hospital.

Two wartime day nurseries were opened on 6 July 1942 to assist mothers with the taking up of war jobs particularly those working in the factories making armaments for the war effort. One nursery was in Caverstede Road run by matron, Miss Cooper, and the other in London Road run by matron, Miss Folker. The ladies from the WVS offered to make special nursery clothes to be worn by the children solely at the establishments. Women in full time positions would be given preference. The nurseries were open between 7.30 am and 8 pm, and could accommodate forty children aged from 7 weeks old up to 5 years. The cost was a shilling a day, including food. The *Peterborough Advertiser* of 10 July 1942 reported that the Mayor had formally opened the nursery at Paston and that although it was a great day for Peterborough, it was deplorable that women should have to go out on war work. 'For a shilling a day, mothers can leave their children of from a few weeks old in the care of trained nurses while they go to their work of helping to win the war, and may be sure that everything possible will be done for their happiness and well-being.' One nursery nurse, formerly from one of the poorer parts of London who had come to work at Paston claimed that come the end of the day, the children did not want to go home because these Tom Thumb children's homes were a paradise thanks to the furnishings, equipment, understanding and cheerfulness of the staff.

A very sad inquest was held on 14 April 1944 into the death of a 9-year-old boy who had been accidentally shot by his friend. Roland Trevor Dixon, only son of Mr. and Mrs. Dixon, of 57 Montague Road had been playing with his next door neighbour Raymond Scoble, aged around 12, in their adjoining front gardens when a shot had been said to have rung out. The mother found her son injured and obtained help from the Paston Lane First Aid post, but it was too late as he had died. It was found that Raymond Scoble's father was a Captain in the Home Guard and somehow the child had obtained his revolver.

Later that year there was another shooting incident, this time involving a soldier and his wife. Arthur William Ilett of Bayne's Yard, Wood Street, was arrested on a charge of intent to do his wife bodily harm by shooting. The Northamptonshire Regiment soldier had been given compassionate leave from his post in Italy because of trouble in the home – his wife had taken up with an Allied soldier and was now in a certain condition. The defendant admitted drunkenly firing the revolver to frighten his wife after arriving home from Italy and finding a proportion of the home missing and the children in an unsatisfactory condition. He was bound over by the magistrates court on 20 December 1944 for twelve months and forced to hand over his revolver.

The Brookwood Memorial, standing in the Southern end of the Canadian part of the Brookwood Military Cemetery near Pirbright army training centre commemorates 3,500 men and women from the Commonwealth Forces 'to whom the fortunes of war denied a known and honoured grave'. The memorial was unveiled by the Queen on 25 October 1958. Roberta Alice Warwick a Sister in the Queen Alexandra's Imperial Military Nursing Service Reserve, 266463, died aged 40 on 12 February 1944. Miss Warwick was from Queen's Walk in Peterborough, daughter of Charles Joseph and Anne Almond Warwick, and was listed in the *London Gazette* as having earned a commission as a Sister on 8 April 1943. Miss Warwick died on the SS *Khedive Ismail* along with seventy-six other service women, the largest loss of service women in the history of the Commonwealth nations, when it was sunk by a Japanese submarine near the Maldives after leaving Mombasa bound for Colorado. It was the third largest mercantile disaster in the Second World War and the worst involving British service women with 77 lost in total.

CHAPTER SIX

Health and Poverty in Peterborough

Betsey Rist of Peterborough would have been considered a vagrant, an unsettled poor woman in a continual state of movement from one property to another. Elizabeth Rist was born in Yaxley near Peterborough in 1850. She moved frequently within an area of a few miles from street to street. Her family were also frequently in court, her father claimed damages when her sister was seduced, her brother Isaac committed bigamy, and there was an association with bodysnatching. Betsey married John Ashworth in 1874 and under her married name of Elizabeth Ashworth, Betsey was regularly in court for assault, damage, malicious wounding and stealing, and was labelled as a prostitute. Such was the law at the time, that if a woman debased herself by being drunk, displayed 'poor behaviour', or was out on the streets after 10 pm in Peterborough, she could be arrested; as far as the authorities were concerned, a respectable woman would not be out on her own at night.

Betsey was first labelled as a prostitute in 1878 when she stole 7 shillings. In 1881 she was jailed for unlawfully and maliciously wounding her husband. In her 1892 conviction for stealing, she was given five months hard labour and her trade was listed as a 'prostitute'. Her criminal life appears to have begun four years after marrying John Ashworth; he was convicted also – of assaulting her. In 1901, John appeared on the census as living at the Peterborough

Workhouse and Betsey was recorded as living alone in City Road. It is thought that Betsey entered the Kesteven County Asylum not long after this and died some short time later.

The Kesteven County Asylum was a mental institution in the parish of Quarrington, Lincolnshire. The Lunacy Act of 1845 pushed for every county to have their own asylum and to not send out paupers to other asylums. However patients from Peterborough were frequently sent to Kesteven as other asylums were often full. Asylum blocks included wards for acute and generalized cases, chronic and difficult cases, a block for 'idiots and imbeciles' and a block for epileptics. The lists of patients in the census entries for asylums in the nineteenth century makes you realise how all walks of life were represented here, from the richest private patients, to those deemed to be 'pauper patients'. In the 1871 census for the Northampton General Lunatic Asylum a baroness, governesses, the wife of a publisher and a hospital matron were all inmates.

Women were more likely to be asylum inmates than men as they were seen as more susceptible to disease and illness. Basis for the diagnosis of insanity could include hysteria, depression, anxiety and stress. The asylum was seen as the convenient and socially acceptable excuse for inappropriate and potentially scandalous behaviour, and people were frequently hidden away within their walls. Postnatal depression, overwork, hormones or infidelity were triggers for anyone who could persuade two doctors to sign certificates of insanity to put someone away. These institutions were surrounded by high walls to prevent escapes and there was always a cemetery within to bury anyone who lost their life during their stay.

The Poor Law Guardians had their own Union Workhouse built in Thorpe Road. The workhouse held 200 people but still had to offer considerable outdoor relief despite the fact that most areas had officially abolished this assistance as 12,000 vagrants were found to need the help of the Guardians in 1863. The need for out-relief continued in Peterborough until the Board of Guardians was eventually terminated and the County Council took over in 1930. Outdoor relief was a programme of social welfare and poor relief. Assistance was given in the form of money, food, clothing or goods to alleviate poverty without the need for the recipient to enter the workhouse. In contrast, those who received indoor relief were required to enter some form of institution, workhouse or poorhouse. If you were admitted, you would be interviewed, given a bath and be issued with a workhouse uniform. Your own clothes would be washed and returned to you when you left the establishment. Inmates were examined by the medical officer upon admission. Those who were capable were expected to work with women carrying out domestic duties.

In November 1855, at Thorpe Road Union Workhouse, there were 80 men, 79 women and 140 children registered. The standard of comfort had to be kept lower than for labourers in work, so the infirmary beds were comprised of rushes on a wooden frame that had a sacking bottom. Those who resided in Thorpe Road were generally orphans, the elderly, the insane and physically feeble. The standard payments per week in Peterborough were: 2*s* 6*d* for a single man, 3*s* for a man and wife, and 6*d* issued per child. Half of the monies paid were in kind, with tickets for an appropriate value handout to be used at certain bakers and grocers within the city. In the main accommodation block the males were housed to the west and the females to the east, the infirmary block was on the northern side of the site. A fever ward with 20 beds and a chapel were added in 1864, followed by two vagrant wards in 1870. By 1874 the workhouse could accommodate approximately 370 inmates. Further additions to Thorpe Road Union Workhouse were the Master's House in 1913, the new infirmary, known as St John's Hospital, and a nurses' home in 1932.

The Poor Law Board published a return of all the names of workhouse inmates who had been resident for a continuous period of five years or longer. At Thorpe Road these were:

Emma Woodrow: 6 years, 6 months, Weak Mind
Elizabeth Layton: 12 years, Weak Mind
Jane Bigley: 13 years, Weak Mind
Catharine Smith: 8 years, Weak Mind
Letitia Bingham: 10 years, Weak Mind
Mary Ann Northfield: 5 years, Four illegitimate children.

In the 1881 census only Elizabeth Layton was still resident and was listed as being 57 years of age and an 'imbecile'. An imbecile was a person of moderate to severe difficulties or chronic dementia with a mental age of three to seven years – they could perform simple tasks under supervision and have some degree of communication. In comparison, an idiot was considered to have severe difficulties or congenital mental deficiency and have no form of communication or sense of danger.

In 1865 the workhouse was accused of starving its inmates to death. The inquiry that was held found that those inmates concerned were aged in their 70s and had died of pneumonia. A few years later the Guardians of the Peterborough Union Workhouse placed an advertisement in the *Peterborough Standard* in March 1871 requesting a contract to provide articles for the male inmates such as men's clothes, felt hats by the dozen and pairs of braces, and for the female residents: trimmed bonnets, strong stays, Flannel of Lancashire House, and high boots made of a good kip leather with jean lining. Patterns of the articles and tenders along with the names of two sureties were to be sent to the workhouse before 10 am on Wednesday, 6 April. These items could well be fashioned by women working in cottage industries from home which would then be sent on to their employer and then onwards to the workhouse.

During 1874, a schoolmaster and mistress were appointed. In 1880, at Christmas, the workhouse children travelled in wagons accompanied by their master, mistress and schoolmistress to be entertained by the Honourable Charles Wentworth Fitzwilliam at Milton. At the hall, a large room was decorated, and tea was served for the children at 2.15 pm. They were given tarts, jam, plum cake, bread and butter, and pies. After they had finished eating, the workhouse children were able to play in the park before they were given further treats of milk, oranges, buns and biscuits. They sang some songs and thanked their hosts. Presents were then distributed with each child being given a card, sweets and oranges. Each boy received a large trumpet and each girl was given a doll. There were further Christmas celebrations at the workhouse itself which were provided through the kindness of the guardians. The 206 inmates were served by well-known names when they sat down to a dinner of roast beef and Yorkshire puddings at 1 pm followed by pudding and ale. There was a much decorated Christmas tree which was surrounded by 250 gifts.

In 1885 it was agreed at a Poor Law conference that some of the workhouse children could attend local schools and subsequently there were only fifteen girls and twenty-five boys left to teach within the workhouse itself. Mrs. Nuttall, the institution's teacher, therefore requested a testimonial so that she could apply for an alternative post. This was granted because the fifteen girls could attend city schools and the boys could have their own schoolmaster. Mrs. Nuttall left after the examinations had been completed, and rather than only the girls going to attend to the local city schools, the governors decided that all the children could attend in order 'to remove (them) from the influence of pauperism and give them a start without the stigma of early life', as reported in the *Peterborough Standard*. At the turn of the century the children became separated and placed into cottage homes; in 1907 there were four of these houses, two in Midland Road and two in South Parade. Cottage homes usually housed 'problem' children and were an alternative for pauper children to the physical conditions and detrimental influences of the workhouse. Each cottage home could house between twelve and thirty children at a time. In 1924, the union operated cottage homes at Alderman's Drive and at Midland Road. Alderman's Drive cottage home housed up to 10 children and the superintendent there was a Miss M. Mirkitt, whereas Midland Road cottage home was run by Miss A.M. Middleton and accommodated 22 children.

In Cumbergate in 1903, a row of old almshouses, dating from 1835, and a house of correction were demolished and replaced by Miss Pear's almshouses. They were named after Miss Frances Pears, the Edwardian daughter of a Peterborough draper who had left a legacy of £5,000 in her will of 1901. Frances Pear was born in 1842 and moved to Peterborough with her family. She was a middle class lady thanks to her father's successful business. She lived in a house known as Bennithorpe on The Crescent. While Miss Pears was alive she was known to offer both her time and money to support good causes, one of which was to help raise enough money to install 44 new stalls in Peterborough Cathedral. Miss Pears died on 1 December 1901 and, after leaving money to her family, friends and servants, she left: £1,000 for a second curate, £1,000 for the Peterborough infirmary, money towards Christian charities and lastly the £5,000 for the Cumbergate almshouses to be rebuilt. The building is now used as an Italian restaurant and is identifiable by a blue plaque on the wall.

Thanks to industrialisation and the arrival of the railways, the speedy growth of the population brought with it a public health problem which was thought to have died out – typhoid. The drainage and water systems in Peterborough were still of medieval standards and in drier weather, the wells had very little water in them; this is when deaths from typhoid would occur. In the first year of Incorporation in 1874, the Medical Officer of Health reported that, 'typhoid fever is endemic of New England at present. Yesterday I visited thirty cases of this disease there.' The Feoffees maintained sock wells that were sunk into gravel and provided a water supply to the city, but in 1874 the Corporation took over responsibility for the city's amenities.

Within the first six years of Incorporation, the city spent over £200,000 on both water and sewerage for a population of 22,000, but thanks to the foresight and planning, this meant that very little else had to be done to these facilities for the next fifty years. Communal and personal cleanliness also vastly improved within the Peterborough district with Mr Jolly, the Medical Officer of Health, reporting in 1906 that 'the dwellers in these homes are rapidly becoming converted to the belief in the efficacy of soap and water.' The collection of household refuse was now carried out by the council and in 1910 the carts had covers added to them, but the Medical Officer of Health in 1907 complained that hawkers of fish, meat and vegetables were still throwing offal and food waste into the gutters.

During the hundred-year period covered by this book Peterborough had sporadic cases of smallpox, but the diseases that caused the main problem of the city, mainly affecting children, were scarlet fever, diphtheria and tuberculosis. In 1918, Influenza, also known as Spanish Flu, affected Peterborough and was the cause of 88 deaths during a year. This could have been much worse as it was one of the most deadly epidemics in human history. Many soldiers returning home from France were particularly susceptible because they already suffered from things like malnutrition, overcrowding within the medical camps and hospitals, massive troop movements and simply poor hygiene. Those that were affected were sent to the convalescing hospitals, such as Whitehall in Sawtry, under the care of the Red Cross nurses.

John Whitwell was a founding member of the sewerage committee. At each board meeting evidence was presented of the current major problems such as stoppages in the sewers, cesspool problems and drains in poor condition. The cesspool in the national school was reported as overflowing, the infirmary had a faulty drain and in the Long Causeway, the *Peterborough Advertiser* reported 'a particularly offensive effluvium' in 1866. The Peterborough Improvement Commissioners Sewerage Committee Minutes of 1851 reported that there was a row of houses containing over forty inhabitants and there was only one privy.

At the start of the nineteenth century, medical care was virtually non-existent for those on a low income. The Peterborough Public Dispensary, which provided outpatient medical treatment and advice to patients – medical care for the poor – was established in 1815 and was situated at the end of Cowgate. The latter then moved from Cowgate to Milton Street sometime in the 1840s. The Union Workhouse with an attached infirmary had opened in 1837, however the standard of care was poor and it soon became evident that the workhouse was unsuitable for the sick. Workhouse infirmaries were run under the Poor Law regime. Lunatics could not be held in a workhouse for more than fortnight and the free medical care was not available to those outside. Every Poor Law Union had a medical officer but the nursing was in the hands of other inmates, most of whom could not read,

In 1850, the infirmary could still be found in Milton Street and was very well used. In 1856 it was necessary to move to larger accommodation and so the infirmary relocated once more, this time to a grand town house in Priestgate, which was known at that time as 'Squire Cook's House'. In June 1928, it was again decided that the current premises were too small and everything was relocated to the Peterborough and District War Memorial Hospital with the former building becoming the City Museum and Art gallery in 1931 after refurbishment.

The city's isolation hospital was also known as the sanatorium and was built on the site of Low Farm, a former grange of the chamberlain of Peterborough Abbey. The sanatorium was opened in 1901 for patients with infectious diseases with thirty-two beds. The Matron, Miss Skinner, ran the hospital along with six nurses and five domestics. The hospital provided treatment for infectious diseases such as smallpox, diphtheria, typhoid, cholera and polio. Tuberculosis was also extremely common at this time. The sanatorium offered good nutrition, rest, clean air and mineral springs.

The Bishop's Palace was opened in 1918 due to the large numbers of injured soldiers coming through from the front; trains were regularly stopping at both the North and East railway stations. It soon became clear that the Priestgate Infirmary couldn't cope with the new arrivals so part of the Bishop's Palace was opened up as a hospital on 7 September 1918 to provide medical care in clean, comfortable surroundings.

The War Memorial Hospital cost between £70,000 and £80,000 to build and was officially opened on 14 June 1928 by Field Marshal Sir William Robertson. It was a voluntary hospital thanks to public contributions made after the First World War. The Children's Hospital to the south was opened the following year. When the hospital opened it had six wards in three blocks. By 1940, the hospital was recognised as a training school for nurses under the General Nursing Council and the nurses' homes were located at Midland Road and Sutton House on Alderman's Drive.

By the end of the Second World War, it had been decided by the health board that the Memorial Hospital could longer cope with the number of Peterborough's residents and it was decided that a new hospital was needed. In 1948 the War Memorial Hospital was transferred to the National Health Service and came under the Peterborough and Stamford Hospitals Management Committee of the East Anglian Regional Hospitals Board. This hospital was closed in 1968 and was replaced by the Peterborough District Hospital which was built on the site of the former Thorpe Road workhouse.

The Maternity Hospital was at Thorpe Hall, a large hall with extensive grounds, formerly owned by the Fitzwilliams from 1943 onwards. The Gables, in Thorpe Road, was a former private home for the Beeby family until 1947 when it too became a maternity hospital. Births in the workhouse were registered and also recorded in the workhouse's own register of births. In 1904, in order to reduce stigma, the birth registration did not state workhouse but gave an address such as 1, Glapthorne Road for the Oundle workhouse. Deaths were also recorded similarly, relatives could collect the body and arrange burial in their home parish. If not, burial was arranged by the Guardians. Widows and daughters would have to apply to be allowed to collect their relative's effects.

Marion Ann Dunn, a mother with young children, was killed by a train on Crescent Crossing in 1880 and this led to a report into safety around the railways. The railway company was enforced to place a gateman on the eastern side of the crossing until a more permanent form of safety could be put in place.

The name of Alice McKenzie was reported in the *Peterborough Advertiser* on 19 January 1889. Alice had been taken to court having been charged with begging in a butcher's shop on Long Causeway. Women often begged to avoid going into the workhouse and in order to feed themselves, their family or their addictions. On the 15th, she had purchased a pennyworth of chitterlings, consumed them quickly and asked for some more for free and was subsequently arrested. The *Peterborough Standard* described the incident:

> On the 15th of January, in the present year, about a quarter to 10 o'clock in the morning, Alice McKenzie went into the shop of Mrs Popp, pork butcher, Long Causeway and purchased a sausage,

which she ate ravenously, and used most disgusting and abusive language to Mrs Popp, so that she was obliged to call in the assistance of PC Smith, who took her to the police station on a charge of begging.

Alice was released without a conviction, having been given a caution by the magistrate; she was found dead six months later in Whitechapel – potentially the eighth and final victim of the infamous Jack the Ripper.

During the last few months of 1888, at least five prostitutes had been murdered on the streets of the East End of London by what was thought to be the same hand. Each woman had had their throat cut and most had been mutilated in a gruesome brutal way. These murders had prompted a widescale murder hunt, but the Metropolitan Police never found the killer.

Alice McKenzie, the victim of the murder was about 45 years of age, and was about 5ft 4in tall. She had brown hair and eyes and a fair complexion.

The Western Times published this description, which had been circulated by the authorities, on Thursday, 18 July 1889 –

> She is believed to have been of the 'unfortunate' class, but has not yet been identified.
>
> She wore a red staff bodice, patched under the arm and a brown staff skirt. She also had on a linsey petticoat, black stockings, buttoned boots, and a Paisley shawl; but no hat or bonnet.
>
> One peculiarity in the description may serve for purposes of identification: part of the nail on the thumb on the left hand is deficient.

Later published in the same edition of *The Western Times* –

> Several hours elapsed before the woman was identified, but a man named John McCormack came forward during the day and recognised her as Alice Mackenzie with whom he had lived for six or seven years, and who has for some time lodged with him as his wife at a common lodging house in Gun Street kept by a man named Tenpenny.

> McCormack stated that he did not know whether the deceased had been married, and that the reason of her going out last night was that they had had a slight quarrel, and that she had never, to his knowledge, been out late at night previously.
>
> McCormack speaks of her as a hard-working woman and seems very much upset at the occurrence.

Alice was thought to have been resident in the East End of London in 1874 and worked in the area as washerwoman and charlady. One in three women in the Whitechapel district were forced to supplement their income frequently by selling sexual favours. Drunkenness was also common in this area and Alice was no exception. She had gained her nickname of 'Clay Pipe Alice' as she had a habit of wearing a clay pipe over her ear.

In 1883 Alice had met her common-law husband John McCormack (or Bryant). He was an Irish porter to some Jewish tailors who were based in Hanbury. The two of them lived at Mr. Tenpenny's Doss House in Gun Street.

The *Peterborough Express* reported 'Alice McKenzie, ... a few years ago resided at Peterborough and will probably be known to some of the residents of Boongate and its vicinity.' Boongate, one of the less salubrious areas of Peterborough, was riddled with poverty and was an occasional haunt of prostitutes.

Her final hours were detailed at the inquest following her death, of which the records can be found in the National Archives. On Tuesday 16 July 1889, John McCormarck returned home drunk to their lodgings at around 4 pm and went to bed. He had given Alice money to pay their rent and buy food, but she went out for a drink and was seen at 7 pm at the Royal Cambridge Music Hall. Alice was witnessed two hours later returning to the lodging house by fellow lodger Elizabeth Ryder, who stated that Alice appeared drunk, Mrs Ryder also saw Alice leave again a little while later after the alleged argument with her common-law husband about her squandering of the rent and food money. Later at 11.40 pm a woman called Margaret Franklin was sitting with two friends at the junction of Flower and Dean Street and greeted Alice, who was walking hurriedly; Alice replied saying that she could not stop to chat. Alice was described as wearing a light coloured shawl around her shoulders and was missing a bonnet.

Police officers patrolling the Whitechapel district walked through Castle Alley just after midnight and saw nothing out of the ordinary. PC Andrews returned through the alley at around 12.45 am and discovered the body of a woman lying on the pavement with two stab wounds in her neck, her skirts lifted revealing that her abdomen had been mutilated. In her possession was a clay pipe and a bronze farthing. Alice was found to have been murdered by 'person or persons unknown'. A man did come forward claiming to have murdered Alice, a William Wallace, but he had just arrived from South Africa and could not have possibly committed the crime. The authorities were in disagreement as to whether Alice had been murdered by Jack the Ripper. The head of the CID for the Metropolitan Police, Sir Robert Anderson; Doctor George Bagster Phillips; and the Coroner, were unconvinced. Doctor Thomas Bond, however, who was one of the key medical experts on the case and who had examined the majority of the Ripper victims, and the Assistant Commissioner James Monro of the Metropolitan Police, both believed that Alice had been killed by the Ripper.

Other sad deaths shocked the local community. In 1855 there was a severe frost which had frozen the river to such an extent that people were able to stand and skate on it. Sadly the ice thawed quite rapidly and two boys were drowned despite the best efforts of six men who went to the rescue. The men were able to retrieve the bodies and John Gates recorded the fatalities as accidental loss of life thanking the men for their assistance. *A History of Peterborough Parish Church of St John's* describes how difficult life could be in 1857. The Baptist records of St John's Church in the centre of Peterborough show that Vincent, the son of Stephen and Emma Card, was born on 21 March and baptised at home on 27 March due to 'danger of death'. Records show that the boy died before the end of the month and was carried to church on 12 April, where Thomas Seed carried out sacred ceremonies and prayers. Later, on 5 February 1872, the details of an inquest into the death of an unknown male infant whose body had been found in a privy cesspool in Marholm was published in the *Peterborough Advertiser*. The post mortem revealed that the infant had died some six weeks previously, but it was impossible to tell whether the baby had been born alive or stillborn. At a later quarter session, a servant, Harriet Green, in the employ of Mrs Mann of Helpston, was brought before the judge accused of a 'concealment of a baby at birth'. It was said that Harriet had been complaining of back trouble and had retired to a room some time ago. After the body of the baby was found Harriet denied it was hers, but a soiled apron was discovered in her room. Harriet then admitted that the child was hers and that it had not cried, she had put the baby into a slop bucket and placed it into the privy at the bottom of the garden. Harriet Green was sentenced to three months imprisonment.

In March 1889 there was a tragic death on the Lode in Stanground. Young Susannah Smith, a bright 6-year-old, was playing on the frozen water along with some other children when the ice gave way. Two boys managed to get out, three others were rescued by Charles Hill, George Bains and Mr W. Northcott, but it was only when the ice was broken and the water dragged that Susannah Smith's body was found.

Murder in Peterborough – On 22 August 1914, in School Place, there was an argument between husband and wife, John Francis Eayrs and Sarah Ann Eayrs (his former housekeeper). Both were aged in their 50s and their neighbours claimed that both drank copiously. Sarah was found with her throat cut and lying face down in her own blood. John was found with his face and shorts covered in blood. His throat was slit but he was still alive and the Police Surgeon, Dr R.W. Jolly, was soon on the scene. He found blood on John's hand and clothing, as well as a bloody knife in his pocket. Although the throat cut was not serious, John was taken first to Peterborough Infirmary. At the murder trial, the jury found John Francis Eayrs guilty of willful murder after just ten minutes and the death sentence was passed.

****

The Fletton Infant Welfare Centre was formed in November 1915 and provided a service that is currently offered today by midwives and health visitors. The aim was to help educate new mothers about caring for their children and to help reduce the infant mortality rate in the city. Within a month of forming the committee, the 10 founders had found a qualified doctor willing to help at the centre and acquired rooms from which to operate. The centre was completely funded by donations. Within a year the infant mortality rate in the area had dropped from 14.1 per cent to 3.5 per cent.

In 1930, the East Ward of Peterborough needed to raise money towards the New Hospital and was £1,711 short of its target so decided to hold a three-day Olde English Fayre. A group of ladies calling themselves the 'Cream of Gentlewomen of the city' ran more than twenty events dressed in period costume using the slogan 'So buy our things, and see our shows, and bring our labours to a close. Then thanks to us, and thanks to you, the Hospital will have its due.'

Hardship, vagrancy and associated poverty were a big issue in Peterborough during this period. In 1885-86 at the end of Edward Vergette's mayoral year, a small banquet was held in order to raise money for 400 blankets to distribute around to poor families. The *Peterborough and Huntingdonshire Standard* had recorded that although the hardship in the city was similar to other towns there was no fund for assistance within Peterborough. Another councillor also supplied 250 loaves to the poor in Boongate but it was reported in the *Standard* that distress had never been so prevalent at this time. Although the guardians of the workhouse were giving out funds to those families whose men were out of work, it was a small pittance. The directors of the Coffee Houses were reported in late February 1886 as handing out soup and bread tickets to the deserving poor. At the same time Earl Fitzwilliam was donating coal but it was discovered that some employed workers were receiving donations of coal while others who had no money or work were having their names crossed off the list.

On 10 November 1943, Beryl Constance pleaded guilty at the Magistrate's Court to the charge of 'sleeping out and not being able to give a good account of oneself'. Beryl had originally travelled from London to March in order to find work, but she had absconded with some money and then been fined for travelling between March and Peterborough without a ticket. She was subsequently arrested in an air raid shelter in the local area having been found sleeping rough, despite her claiming she had a caravan in Westwood; a medical examination suggested that she had been sleeping rough for several weeks and Beryl had sores all over her arms and legs. The magistrates sentenced Beryl to two months in prison and the chairman told her that she would be properly looked after now.

Domestic abuse was not uncommon either: The Stamford Workhouse, on Barnack Street, was the usual site for inquests carried out by the Peterborough Coroner as there needed to be a large room for as many local people as possible to attend, however this inquest was held at the Star Inn on the corner of Star Road and Bishops Road. In 1897, Emma Perrin drowned herself and her toddler in the fen drain at Fengate. She had been the victim of long term domestic abuse at the hands of her husband Edward, and was in despair when she died. At the end of the inquest, her husband was helped to escape out of the rear of the pub and across the fens, as the locals wanted to lynch him. Edward Perrin was never seen in Peterborough again.

The 1853 Criminal Procedure Act (also referred to as the Act for the Better Prevention of Aggravated Assaults upon Women and Children) was the first legislative attempt made to limit the chastisement that a man could give his wife and/or children. Few nineteenth century police would step over the front door threshold unless the violence was extreme or a public nuisance. Under this new legislation a husband could receive a six month sentence for assault but his wife and family could be subject to financial hardship as a result and potentially face some sort of reprisal once the husband/father was released. Later Acts allowed for wives to divorce their husbands based on cruelty and to receive maintenance.

In 1895 the Summary Jurisdiction (Married Women) Act allowed women to separate from their husbands, however this required both parties to be brought before a court and there was much shaming from both parties which could cause embarrassment etc. By the end of the nineteenth century the creation of the National Society for the Prevention of Cruelty to Children and the Associate Institution of Improving and Enforcing the Laws for the Protection of Women helped more cases be brought to the courts, and the law, as well as these societies, helped change both public and opinion about domestic abuse.

CHAPTER SEVEN

Women's Leisure Time in Peterborough

In Peterborough, the last sedan chair was available for hire as late as the 1870s which suggests that the character of the town was slow to feel change until the arrival of the railways. The chairs were not cheap to hire and the men who ran the service were notorious for being argumentative and frequently drunk. The sedan chair service was fantastic for ladies however as it allowed ladies to get about the city while keeping their voluminous skirts dry and free of mud and dirt from the streets. The sedan consisted of a seat inside a cabin that had a detachable roof and was mounted on 2 poles that were carried by 2 men, known as chairmen, with one at the front and one at the rear. Priestgate was the most prestigious residential street in the city and the residents enjoyed watching the ladies and hearing the tittle tattle, using the sedan chairs to get between social events. In the 1869 directory Mr Jackson of St Leonard's Street was listed as a sedan chair operator.

The next option for women to get around the city was by horse bus. The horse buses were first seen in Peterborough in 1857. Mr Chamberlain started a Saturday only service which ran between Market Place and New England. Other operators experimented with horse buses and wagonettes along the same route. In 1896 William Bailey, a leading innkeeper, set up the Peterborough Omnibus Company which operated a large network of horse-bus routes throughout the city.

Later, in 1899, the British Electric Traction Company sought authority for a network of routes to be run by electric trams which would connect the northern suburbs of Newark, Dogsthorpe and Walton with the city centre. These electric trams started running at the end of January 1903 and this continued until 1930. There were however only fourteen tramcars in the fleet and it was a tiny network in comparison to other areas. The first motor buses appeared in Peterborough in 1913 with four Straker Squires, two saloons and two charabancs. These vehicles supplemented the tramways. The first double decker bus arrived in 1924 and not before long the double decker bus managed to get stuck under the Rhubarb Bridge in Lincoln Road, Walton and proved impossible to unstick until a passer-by suggested letting the tyres down! After the tramway stopped running there was soon a large number of buses running services all over Peterborough.

An official bathing spot was opened on the Nene above River Lane, in Oundle, in 1880 and was only open for use during the summer months between May and September. Here the bank was walled and a third of the river was filled with gravel to allow for a summer depth of approximately two to four foot. Wooden cubicles, for changing, were erected behind the towing path. The bathing spot was solely for men's use until a Ladies Day was established in 1923. The bathing spot was used seasonally until the swimming pool was opened.

In 1936 the Peterborough Swimming Pool, otherwise known as the Lido or the Corporation, opened; it had cost £20,800 to build, in today's money around £1.5 million. The Lido was much appreciated during the war years as a place to relax, despite some damage sustained in June 1940 by a German bomb.

Alternative leisure pursuits for women were available on the River Nene in the form of hiring pleasure boats; taking trips along the Nene had always been a popular pastime with the locals. The boats would be secured in the evening and the oars and sails stored in a nearby houseboat overnight. Cycling was also a popular pastime within Peterborough. F. & G.W. Burrows shop at No 57 Westgate next to the Crown Inn was a bicycle dealer.

Central Park, partially completed, was opened to the public in 1877 but admittance was originally by subscription only. In 1900 the cost of summer season tickets was 15/ for families and 5/ for single people. Later in 1908, the Peterborough council took over responsibility for the site on a 999 year lease.

Towards the end of the period covered by this book, Peterborough was earmarked for expansion to meet the needs of an ever-growing population. The twenty-year plan was eventually published in 1951 and included the provision of public recreation spaces.

The Peterborough Choral Society was formed in the Autumn of 1872 after the members of the town's Cathedral Voluntary Choir formed a glee club (part song choral music). The subscription was a penny a week and each individual member could invite one friend to attend two of the main concerts each year.

The Public Library was formed in 1892 and was housed in the Fitzwilliam Hall. In 1905 the library relocated to a new building situated on the Broadway, built with a grant of £6,000, approximately £750,000 today. The new library was opened by the Scottish philanthropist Andrew Carnegie in May 1906 and has since relocated to the Peterborough Central Library in 1990.

On 21 June 1887 celebrations were organised for Queen Victoria's Golden Jubilee. The day, a general holiday, was heralded by the pealing of the bells from St John's and St Mary's churches and the Royal Standard was flown from the Guildhall and other businesses. A regatta was held on the river and then there was a procession led by the Incorporation and three local bands. The parade included a number of decorated vehicles. The people of importance from the city attended a sumptuous banquet at the Great Northern Hotel where the tables inside were decorated with a variety of flowers and ferns. After a number of speeches and toasts were made, the evening concluded at 10 pm after the National Anthem was played. St John's parish church held a service to start the proceedings, there was lunch arranged for the aged poor (1,200) at the Midland Railway Sheds in Thorpe Road, children gathered at Market Place at 2 pm, where the Jubilee Anthem was sung, a procession of 5,000 Sunday and day school children and illuminated cars headed by the mayor, Alderman H.P. Gates headed to the old agricultural showground on Lincoln Road, where sports activities and tea was provided for the children in the Sexton Barn. The rowing club also staged a regatta. Each child (5,000 in total) received a cup or mug engraved with a picture of the Queen and the city's arms. In the evening the streets were illuminated, there was a huge display of fireworks and a magnesium flare was exhibited from Ely Cathedral which could be seen from Peterborough. Among the inmates of the Peterborough workhouse who celebrated the Golden Jubilee were a man and woman who had been in residence at the workhouse when Victoria had ascended to the throne fifty years earlier.

A thanksgiving service was subsequently held at the cathedral on 23 June with the mayor and corporation wearing their official robes. The service was then followed by the mayor's Golden Party. It was reported that on the Jubilee day itself, everything had gone smoothly and that 'the city was prettily decorated with a liberal display of flags, floral devices and loyal mottoes'. Ten years later the Diamond Jubilee was celebrated in 'torrid heat' and the city was equally lavishly decorated.

Prior to the Golden Jubilee festivities, a suggestion was made that every girl and woman in the country, whose name was recorded, should donate a jubilee gift to the Queen of £1 who would decide on what should be financed. Mrs Magee and Mrs Gates headed the local committee for this project.

One summer's day in August 1895, onlookers in the Fletton Recreation Ground watched in horror as a female parachutist fell to her death. Annie (Adelaide) Bassett, aged 36, from the East End in London was experienced in this kind of dare-devil, double-aeronaut jump, having made thirty similar exhibitions in the past. On this day, however, the Victoria smoke balloon, operated by her partner Captain Alfred Norton (a professional aeronaut), became tangled in some trees and telegraph wire, with the parachute device becoming detached from the balloon. Alfred had tried to warn Annie not to jump but instead she misunderstood him and jumped anyway, approximately 70ft, falling to her death. On 5 August, the *Peterborough Advertiser* sensationally described the scene:

> What is this? The balloon lurches – it strikes a tree! Then rolls like a huge aerial porpoise against some telegraph wires. Something is wrong!

Wires detach Mademoiselle's parachute, it falls and hangs umbrella-like downwards. The crowd get anxious. What does it all mean? The two aloft are seen to confer, and – great horrors – Mademoiselle leaps from her perch, her parachute cannot and will not right itself, and she falls, falls like a wounded bird, 200 feet to the ground, with a sickening thud! A thousand voices exclaim 'She's killed'.

The jury at her inquest recommended 'that since no useful purpose is served by these senseless exhibitions at which the lives of the performers are risked, they should be made illegal.'

Katherine (Kitty) Roberts was the only daughter born to Dr Lewis Clayton and Katherine Clayton, the second Freewoman of the City. In her early years Kitty had a promising singing voice, but it soon became apparent that she would not be able to make a professional career from it. Instead she turned to writing, producing and acting in plays in aid of charitable causes. In 1909 she wrote and produced the play *Aldwinkle Pageant*, which was a masque in ten parts covering the periods between 1070 and 1763. She planned a tableau for a large missionary exhibition in 1914, but it was cancelled due to the outbreak of the First World War. Another play, the *Parish Watchman*, was performed in London and was based around the humour of vicarage life. Kitty herself married the Reverend Robert Edwin Roberts in January 1913, he had starred in in the *Aldwinkle Pageant*, and had been a Precentor at the cathedral since 1908. The wedding was an important event locally with over 300 guests invited and the *Peterborough Advertiser* reported that 'rarely has more interest been evinced in a marriage locally.' During the First World War, Kitty's husband was on active service as a Chaplain to the Forces, so she attended the Women's Temperance Meetings in Peterborough and continued being an active citizen when they moved to Knighton, Leicester, assisting with the Mothers' Union there. She and her husband then collaborated on a book called *Peterborough*, part of *The Story of the English Towns* series, published by the Society for the Promoting of Christian Knowledge. The book was dedicated in loving memory of her father, who had been associated with Peterborough Cathedral for some time. Kitty continued writing and assisting with the Mothers' Union for many years after.

Edith Alderman was born on 7 September 1900 at the Bridge House in Thorney, Peterborough. As she grew, Edith was found to have a lovely soprano voice and initially took part in the Thorney Abbey Choir. In 1913 she took the Elementary exam, then later in 1919 sat an exam of the Royal Academy of Music, and in 1920 passed a singing exam at the Guildhall School of Music. Edith then won a scholarship, enabling her to continue studying in London and was able to study all of the musical arts. On one visit home Edith was reported to have taken part in a recital at the Grand Assembly Rooms – 'Miss Alderman, who is a brilliant pupil at the Guildhall School of Music, delighted her audience both by her beautiful voice and pleasing manner and her excellent and comprehensive choice of songs.' She chose the stage name Ena Roscoe when her quickly blossoming career took her away from the theatres in Peterborough to the Drury Lane Theatre in London. She was a leading lady in The Arcadians, she played Cinderella at the People's Palace and starred in *Catherine*, a musical written by Tchaikovsky. She also got to meet Walt Disney who gave her some 18in statues of his Snow White characters and these were given pride of place on her mantelpiece. Ena never had children and passed away in 1994 aged 93.

In the *Peterborough Standard* of 18 February 1911 there was a plea by the Peterborough Women's Unionist Association for the women of the city to 'not fail to come and hear the celebrated Lantern Lecture on South Africa by Councillor A.R. Atkey of Nottingham at the Drill Hall on Thursday next, February 21st at 8 pm'. The Women's Unionist Association was formed in 1908 and was opened to Conservative members who were only interested in the enfranchisement of women. During the First World War, the women of the Union sent thirty parcels a fortnight to prisoners of war. Although all were welcome, the advert did stipulate that the event was for women only. Alternative programmes in the city at this time included *A Wife's Romance* and the *Air Pirates of* 1920, a silent film. Matinees were usually at 2.30 pm and evening films at

6:30 pm, with seats available for 3*d*, 6*d* and 1s (equivalent to 35, 70 pence and £1.45 in today's money)

There were large crowds lining Broad Bridge Street during the coronation celebrations for King George V and Queen Mary on 22 June 1911. The procession was headed by a splendid steam traction engine which was hauling a royal float, a coronation crown with a banner reading 'Long Live the King', and numerous other floats were lined up behind, such as the float belonging to the Pork Butchers Association, with a replica pig standing on straw with the different cuts of pork depicted around the sides of the float.

In 1912, an entire Peterborough family was lost in the Titanic disaster, an event which affected the whole world. Mr and Mrs Sage had moved to Peterborough from King's Lynn and had set up a business in Gladstone Street, a baker's shop and off-licence. Mr Sage decided that the family would be better off relocating to the United States of America to give the children a better life. The ship they had booked was forced to stay in the port because of a coal shortage, so their travel was rescheduled to the Titanic, which was due to make its maiden voyage from Southampton. It was said that Mrs Sage and her daughter had reservations about travelling on the Titanic as they had read the novel by Morgan Robertson, published some fourteen years previously, about the fictional ship 'Titan', which had grounded on an iceberg and subsequently sank. Mr Sage, his wife, five daughters and four sons were among the numerous people who lost their lives in the North Atlantic in 1912.

Sadly accidents could affect the women of Peterborough, for instance: an accidental death occurred on 23 August 1911 on Lincoln Road where Stone Lane and Searjeant Street join. Annie Griffin, aged 18, and her friend Lily Woodcock were larking about on Lincoln Road when Robert Walker was cycling along to get into the city centre. It was said that Annie spotted the cyclist coming and stepped back, however the cyclist swerved and hit her. Annie became unconscious and was taken to a nearby shop. A doctor was called and diagnosed shock and unconsciousness; Annie was then taken to her parents house at 354 Rogers Street. Sadly Annie died at 4.30 am the next day having not regained consciousness. An inquest was held two days later at the New England Workman's Hall, with the cyclist Robert Walker not having been at fault, as reported in the following edition of the *Peterborough Standard*. Much sympathy was found for the parents as Annie was their only child.

A frothblowing group (known as a Vat) was formed at the Campbell Hotel in 1926, having originally been formed in London in 1924 to 'foster the noble Art and gentle and healthy Pastime of froth blowing among Gentlemen of leisure and ex-Soldiers', and was founded by Bert Temple, a wealthy patient and friend of Sir Alfred Fripp as well as an ex-soldier and silk merchant in order to raise large sums of money (initially £100, approximately £5,600 in today's money) for children's charities and hospitals. A good description of the organisation can be found in their handbook: 'A sociable and law abiding fraternity of absorptive Britons who sedately consume and quietly enjoy with commendable regularity and frequention the truly British malted beverage as did their forebears and as Britons ever will, and be damned to all pussyfoot hornswogglers from overseas and including low brows, teetollars and MP's and not excluding nosey parkers, mock religious busy bodies and suburban fool hens all of which are structurally solid bone from the chin up. The idea was to meet up in pubs or clubs to enjoy beer, beef and baccy. Members would be fined for heinous sins such as not wearing the cuff-links. The fines and membership fees would be sent to Sir Alfred and Lady Fripp for the charities. The frothblowers became particularly popular in late 1925 after the editor of the *Sporting Times* started publishing articles on the gatherings of the Order. The Ancient Order of Froth Blowers (AFOB) was very forward thinking in many aspects of its membership and included the ladies who wished to participate even before they got the full vote in the UK. In February 1922 there were 150 Blowers and Fairy Belles who had gathered at the Angel Hotel for supper and a dance.

Male members of the Vat were called Blowers, and female members were called Fairybelles; children and dogs were called Faithful Bow-wows. On 22 February 1927 around 150 Blowers and Fairy Belles congregated at the Angel Hotel for a supper and dance. The frothblowers, who happily consumed beer, had their own song:

The More We Are Together, an adaption of Irving King's *Oh du ivili Augustin*, which was more than likely sung on that night at the Angel Hotel.

> The more we are together, together, together
> The more we are together
> The merrier we'll be.
> For your friends are my friends
> And my friends are your friends,
> And the more we are together,
> The merrier we'll be.

The AFOB's meeting place booklet dated from March/April 1930 lists two Vats as meeting in the Peterborough area: The Grand Hotel Vat, care of Blower F.E. Jordan, and The Windmill Vat, care of Blower F.W.J. Mason, Orton Waterville. The AOFB ceased on 8 December 1931, having more than raised their initial aim of a £100 for children's charities of Sir Alfred Fripp. Sir Alfred Fripp was the chairman of Ye Ancient Order of Froth Blowers and was also a British Surgeon. The charities supported the 'wee waifs' of the East End of London.

The Castor and Ailsworth Women's Institute held its first meeting in 1931. It was organised by the Honorary Georgina Pelham of the 'Cedars'. She was elected president with Mrs Annie Cooke as her Secretary. Until her retirement Mrs Cooke had been Headmistress of Castor Infants' School and village correspondent for three local papers. Concerts and plays by the drama group of the Castor WI in the 1934 Northamptonshire Area Drama Festival were awarded a third class certificate.

In 1935, the Girl Guides of Castor and Sutton were involved in producing Christmas hampers for poor East End families short listed by voluntary social workers.

Bell ringing was a male preserve until the First World War when women were admitted to bell towers as ringers for the first time.

The first of the National Aviation Day Displays organised by Sir Alan Cobham was held on 19 July 1932, just before RAF

Peterborough was officially opened. The *Peterborough Advertiser* ran a competition with free flights as their main prize. One winner of the main prize was Mrs C. Potter of 70 Russell Street, Peterborough – her reaction was 'I have always wanted to go up in an aeroplane. I shan't be a bit afraid.' Mrs Potter was 86 years old! The event was a huge success with large crowds attending to watch the flying displays, to listen to talks by Cobham about the value of air travel and to look at the static exhibitions. The event was subsequently repeated in 1933 before RAF Peterborough officially opened. Once the site was commissioned to the RAF, the organisation decided to hold Empire Air Days and the last of these was held on 15 September 1945 with approximately 7,000 visitors despite the atrocities of the war just past.

The Bridge Fair was always opened by proclamation and this proclamation was only known by the Town Crier whose job it was to read it out. The proclamation below was in use in the 1890s.

> Oyez, oyez, oyez. This is to give notice that the fair called Bridge Fair will be held and kept today, tomorrow and the next day as well as in the County of Huntingdon as Northamptonshire by the order of Her Majesty's Secretary of State dated May 13th 1878 and made in pursuance of the Fairs Act 1878,
>
> Therefore all persons are required to behave themselves soberly and civilly and to pay their respective dues and demands accordingly to the laws of the realm and the rights of the City and borough of Peterborough the owner of aforesaid fair.
>
> God save the Queen.

At the fair in 1864 there were 5,000 beasts, 700 horses, 180 sheep and 75 rams (which sold at mutton prices), whereas in comparison in 1936 there were 150 cattle, 100 horses and no records of sheep. Where the horse fair was has now become the football ground and the beast fair the car park next to the football ground.

In the nineteenth century on a Wednesday and Thursday the town itself was crowded. The railways ran excursion trips from every direction into Peterborough and brought in thousands of people.

Both Bridge Street and the Long Causeway were lined with stalls and Market Place contained a number of agricultural implements which were on display. For the farm labourers in the areas around Peterborough, this was their harvest holiday and an opportunity to spend their harvest money as this was the last holiday before Christmas and the dark days of winter. For the labourer's family Peterborough Bridge Fair offered an opportunity to buy a new coat, winter boots or Sunday suits or frocks.

Sheep breeding was also important locally in the fen lands during the nineteenth century so a ram fair was also held. There was also an agricultural show which is now called the East of England show and this moved to its permanent showground at Eastfield in 1910. Since 1878 the Hound Show has also been run alongside the agricultural show and since 1934 this has been better known as the Royal Foxhound Show.

Between 1846 and 1876, Peterborough had no formal theatre. Some plays and other public performances were held during this period at the Drill Hall on Queen Street, the Fitzwilliam Room at the Angel Hotel and the Wentworth Assembly Rooms. A Fitzwilliam Hall was opened in Park Road which soon became a major venue for theatrical performances and was fitted with a removable surface for roller skating! The Fitzwilliam became known as the Empire and then later the Theatre Royal before becoming re-known as the Empire. The building was re-orientated with a frontage onto a new thoroughfare called the Broadway and soon became the city's main venue for theatrical performances.

Women in Peterborough enjoyed visiting the performances held at the various theatres with many dates occurring on the premises. The Hippodrome was opened in 1907, on the current site of the Tesco store in Broadway and was owned by a London based syndicate. The building had a huge disadvantage in that it had a corrugated iron roof and, as such, in bad weather, heavy hailstone could render the performance inaudible, meaning performances had to be suspended until the weather abated. It was soon sold to Fred Karno, the famous music hall artist and theatrical troupe owner. Karno was born as Frederick Westcott in 1886 and was best known for his showmanship or as an impresario. He brought a number of music hall artists to Peterborough and these were jokingly known as 'Fred Karno's Army' such as Veron Watson and Marie Lloyd. One of his best loved and most enduring artists was Stanley Laurel prior to forming his act with Oliver Hardy. It is thought that Charlie Chaplin also appeared on Karno's billings prior to finding fame and fortune in America.

In 1917 the Grand Theatre on Broadway was showing 'A Royal Divorce' which was a story of Waterloo and was a touring production which visited most of the main theatres around the country. Later in 1932 Ernest Binn's Arcadian Follies toured here as part of their regular showings at the Grand Theatre. The Arcadians were a pierrot troupe, a group of entertainers. Pierrot troupes were popular in Britain during the first half of the twentieth century and would tour around the country particularly to seaside resorts, the troupe being presented by a guy called Ernest Binns. Harry Korris, the comedian, worked alongside the Arcadians for some time. He organised a treat for 1,200 poor children, three years in a row when the Follies were playing at Peterborough and was better known to these children as 'Uncle Harry' between 1933 and 1936.

Jack Bancroft and his family were huge figures of the Peterborough theatre and cinema land, and kept the public entertained particularly through the war years. The Bancroft family took over the Hippodrome theatre in the 1920s after Fred Karno became insolvent. They renamed the theatre the Palace and installed projection equipment thus competing with the Broadway Kinema which was across the street. The Palace offered a full film programme, variety acts, house orchestra and locally produced newsreels. The first talkie film to be shown in Peterborough was at the Palace. Realising the potential for theatre at this time, Jack Bancroft decided to pull down the Hippodrome/Palace and built a brand new theatre which included the latest in design and technology. The new theatre was called The Embassy and opened on 1 November 1937 backing onto the Cattle Market Road. On the opening night Jack Bancroft gave this speech: 'It is exactly twelve years since I came to Peterborough to manage the Palace Cinema and during that time I have tried to please you as patrons and to make your leisure hours as pleasant as possible. During these twelve years I have gained much valuable experience from your constructive criticisms. These criticisms, which are so valuable to progress, together with sincere encouragement from so many of you who are now my friends have helped to bring to life what was once a dream but is now a feat – the Embassy Theatre, Peterborough. I am proud indeed to welcome you here tonight to see opened the doors of a theatre which I feel to be worthy of you all, and of Peterborough. I shall endeavour with your help to offer you only the highest standard that the Theatre can produce. My companies offer you the best possible luxury and comfort in this their new theatre and the way is now open for you in entertainment on a scale never before attempted in Peterborough. We do however need your cooperation and if you on your part continue to give us the wonderful support with which you have favoured us in the past, the Embassy Theatre will become the centre of theatrical entertainment for the whole of the Eastern Counties and a valuable asset to the City.'

The opening production was '1066 and all that'. London productions could easily be staged at the Embassy because of the size of the stage and the proscenium was only slightly smaller than at the London Palladium. The opening night was packed full of people wishing to see the celebrities on stage and the nearby car parks were packed full of coaches bringing people from nearby villages as a night out at the Embassy would be the highlight of the week.

Other cinemas in Peterborough included:

- the Kinema or Gaumont which opened in 1910, was purpose built for the role and it was under the control of various national entertainment corporations.
- The City Picture House, which opened in 1927, could show live productions and was the first cinema in the city to stage a feature length talkie.

- The Odeon theatre which was sited next to the Theatre Royal and Empire in Broadway opened in September 1937 was a hugely successful ultra modern entertainment house.
- Between the mid 1920s and 1950s there were a number of suburban cinemas thanks to the popularity of the cinema. One of these was a converted social centre formerly used by employees of the Great Northern Railway at the junction of Occupation Street and Gladstone Street in New England. Named the New England Cinema, some attendees may have had a disadvantage because the roof support pillars partially obscured the screen nonetheless many courting couples came to take advantage of the dark warm back row. Another suburban cinema was the Woodston Cinema on Palmerston Road in Woodston which was in a converted brewery that still retained its chimney and opened in March 1920. The Princess cinema opened in July 1929 in Millfield at the junction of Lincoln Road and Northfields Road.

Peterborough never had a purpose built music hall but did have a number of venues that could support such acts. Marie Lloyd (1870–1922) was one such major star who came to perform in the city. A master of ceremonies once introduced her with the following words 'Marvellous merrie Marie…tasty, trippy, twiggy, timely, tempting, toothsome, transcendent, trim, tactical, twinkling, triumphal and tantalalising!'

On 12 February 1928 a concert was held in aid of the War Memorial Hospital by Daisy Strickson. In the first half pieces by Chopin, Bach, Monti, Sehira and Weber were played before the five-minute interval. In the second half pieces by Wagner, Liszt, Carey and Chopin were played. A closing piano and organ duet performed by Daisy Strickson and Frank C. Olsen of Wagner's Athemest du Nicht.

On the weekend of 9 June 1929, Britain's Railway Queen, Miss Edna Best, visited Peterborough, staying at Mrs Cullup's of Gladstone Street. Miss Best was 'engaged on a mission of helping to promote peace in industry and cooperation among railwaymen of all countries'.

An old picture postcard suggests that on 9 November 1934, the Fletton United football ground was the venue for a ladies match between the staff of Peterborough Cinemas and Marks & Spencer. The profits from the match were to go to Mayor A.E. Fletcher's Unemployment Fund with admission being charged at 6d for adults and 3d for children.

Hollywood star Clark Gable was often sighted in the centre of Peterborough during 1943, in pubs such as the Blue Peter and The Wheatsheaf in Alwalton, as he was making a recruiting film for aircraft gunners at nearby RAF Polebrook. He flew five combat missions as an observer gunner in a B-17 Flying Fortress between May and September 1943. Girls were so excited to see him and try to get his autograph. The base had been turned over to the United States Army Air Forces (USAAF) the previous year and Gable had joined the 351st Bomb Group which had been sent here. During his time at Polebrook, Gable earned the Air Medal and Distinguished Flying Cross for his efforts. He caused quite a stir amongst the ladies when walking to the American Red Cross Club in City Road.

CHAPTER EIGHT

Active Citizens in Peterborough

The temperance movement was a mass movement in the late nineteenth century. In Peterborough, it was formed as an attempt to stop local workers spending all of their wages on drink so that families, wives and children could have a better life away from the evils of drink. It was hoped that temperance would reduce poverty and violence within poor families. In 1877 a meeting was held by the United Alliance (Temperance) Society. The society supported legislation against drink and advocated 'Sunday' closing for shops which the bishop supported. It was recognised that alcohol was freely available at all times during the nineteenth century and many working people used alcohol as a relief from their life of poverty and working in dangerous and unhealthy conditions. The Temperance Society were keen to try to work with the council and the magistrates so that the alcohol licences for the Bridge Fair could be withheld. At a council meeting this recommendation was made along with further restrictions on the extension of the sale of liquor at public houses in the town for the duration of the fair. The mayor objected strongly to this, and it was pointed out that this restriction would also affect Huntingdonshire which could mean different hours on different sides of the river. The mayor became so incensed that he left his seat and went to sit with the aldermen. The magistrates decided to continue with licences as they were and granted the fairground booths extensions to allow opening between 6:15 a.m. and 6 p.m., the hours for the city inns were to continue as usual.

An opinion of support for Sunday closing appeared in the *Peterborough Standard* dated 11 September 1880 and stated that the ease of getting drink increased the temptation to excessive home consumption, especially among the wives and daughters of artisans and labourers.

The Temperance Society went on in 1882 to erect an iron building on Lincoln Road opposite the turning to Russell Street at a cost of £500 to be used as a coffee tavern. The tavern was opened by the Dean of the cathedral in the presence of Dr. Ackland of Oxford. These two characters were hoped to be seen as proof of the reality of the Temperance Society and that action would be taken to ensure that coffee taverns would be serious rivals to public houses.

The Church of England temperance mission held a meeting at the temperance hall in Boroughbury in March 1883 and arranged to have a second tavern erected six months later. This was built by the coffee shop company at the junction of City and New Road. Another red letter day was the day of opening and the Dean performed the ceremony while supporters and friends of the temperance mission watched. The Dean's address reiterated that the aim of these coffee taverns was to ensure that there was a check on the excessive consumption of intoxicating substances which causes much misery and deprivation. The Bishop followed up these new ventures by writing to the London and provincial press about the grievous sin of intemperance. He believed that in under 30 years of work by earnest Christian men that the evil of drink could be suppressed.

Temperance work was a very popular activity in the nineteenth century, however, the majority of the activists were upper class people trying to tackle working class. Those that saw themselves as 'gentlemen of the city' believed it was their duty to challenge the opening hours of the public houses but they had little or no understanding of the lives of the citizens they were trying to change.

Peterborough's Women's United Total Abstinence Council, or WUTAC, held its first official meeting under the presidency of Lady Mary Glyn on 5 November 1908 at the Palace. The WUTAC's aim was to promote clean living and temperance to the citizens of Peterborough. They wanted to turn people away from the evils of drink as they saw that one of the causes of hardship was alcohol abuse. Peterborough had many public houses which working men could easily access and thus quickly spend their household's weekly outcome, leaving the family short. Drunken husbands may also turn to violence once at home and their wives could be their first target so the WUTAC wanted to create a service as an alternative to alcoholic drink that would be easily available to these workers. The Council also organised charitable or promotional work and events in the city and formed links with other temperance and religious organisations such as the Salvation Army.

A mass meeting was organised with the WUTAC and the temperance movement which would take place at the Corn Exchange:

> In support of the above Message
> A Mass Meeting
> WILL BE HELD IN THE
> CORN EXCHANGE PETERBOROUGH
> ON WEDNESDAY, DECEMBER 8TH
> At 3 o'clock. The chair will be
> Taken by
> THE LORD BISHOP OF PETERBOROUGH
> Speeches will be delivered by
> THE MAYOR OF PETERBOROUGH
> Commissioner ADELAIDE COX
> Of the Salvation Army
> YOU and YOUR friends will be
> HEARTILY WELCOME
> ADMISSION FREE
> A collection will be made to
> Defray expense, surplus given
> To Soldiers & Sailors Funds

One of the first pieces of charitable work that WUTAC carried out was to purchase a coffee van and use it within the Peterborough Market Place to encourage the local men away from the public houses and inns. At the start of the First World War, the Council renovated a building to be used as a rest room at the Great Eastern Station for the use of soldiers and sailors passing through Peterborough on their way to or from the Front. The rest room opened on Christmas Eve 1915 and became very popular with the troops passing through.

The Peterborough Standard reported on 15 January 1916 that 'The following figures testify to the usefulness of the Soldiers' and Sailors' Rest Home which has been fitted up at the G.E. Railway Station. The Home was opened on Christmas Eve, and during the first nine days the numbers of soldiers and sailors upon whom its hospitality was bestowed was 321, an average of 36 a day.' Letters of thanks and postal orders for food were sent to the ladies running the rest room such as 10 shillings from a 2nd Lieutenant of the Black Watch which was to pay for food that some of his men had while travelling through.

Mr. Bodger supervised the rest room at the East Station, together with the Bishop of Peterborough and Lady Mary Glyn. Mr. Bodger frequently undertook social and religious work within the city including being on the Board of Guardians, the Church of England and the Peterborough Branch of the London City Mission. After the war ended the Rest Room closed but the Council continued to hold meetings and run the coffee van for some years after.

First calls for Women's Suffrage in Northamptonshire came from Peterborough via a petition on 15 April 1869. A further petition was submitted in June of the same year with more following in 1870 and 1871. In March 1872, another petition was signed, this time at a meeting on Women's Suffrage chaired by Benjamin Taylor, an ally in the campaign. Taylor chaired another meeting regarding women and the vote in 1873 where Caroline Biggs, a Leicester born Executive Member of the National Society of Women's Suffrage and Emily Spender, feminist novelist from Bath, spoke as part of a Suffrage tour.

The next meeting on the subject of Women's Suffrage in Peterborough was chaired by the Reverend Alexander Murray, Minister of the Congregational Chapel on Westgate and took place in December 1874. The speaker at this meeting was Helena Downing, an Irish socialist, and the minister was so moved by the speech that he subscribed to the Central Committee of the National Society for Women's Suffrage. Helena also spoke at the next meeting in the city in 1882, alongside Maye Dilke who was the author of the book *Women's Suffrage: A treatise on equality*.

On 27 May 1910 at the Grand Assembly Rooms on Wentworth Street, the first Women's Social and Political Union (WSPU) meeting took place in Peterborough. Tickets for this meeting could be obtained from Caster's book shop. The chair was a Dr Glaisher from Trinity College in Cambridge and he was supported by Mrs Rackham, Miss Ward and Miss Corbett. The meeting was held to examine the objectives of the society as a constitution and the campaigning body. At the meeting it was stated that the WSPU was more appealing to people's sense of justice with regards to votes for women and the National Union had gone from 50 to 130 branches in 3 years so it was hoped that a Suffrage Society could appear in Peterborough very soon.

In 1911, Helen Craggs became the first WSPU organiser for Peterborough, 8 years after the WSPU had been established, and she worked from 14 Cromwell Road as a Secretary for the Union. She was answerable to Grace Roe in Ipswich. Craggs was one of the militant suffragettes that had been arrested during riots in London during 1910, having joined the WSPU in 1908 under the name of Helen Millar, she had been involved in chalking pavements and handing out literature in the Peckham area of London. She also hid in the roof of the Paragon Theatre in Whitechapel where Lloyd George was due to speak and then burst out shouting about votes for women. Craggs was very close to Emmeline Pankhurst's son Harry, who suffered from polio and died in 1910. She did not spend long in Peterborough as a secretary and was soon replaced by Mrs Fordham in 1912.

Emmeline Pankhurst had previously spoken in Peterborough at the first meeting of the Peterborough branch of the Independent Labour Party in 1905 but visited again in 1911. An anonymous article was published in the *Peterborough Advertiser* on 11 February 1911 about a meeting held by the WSPU:

> To the average man and woman, the lull in political activity following the General Election, is welcomed as a merciful release and relief from exhausting exertions, once more to the conditions of normal existence. One organisation there is, however, which never slumbers of sleep [sic], and whose members seem inspired with the principle of ceaseless activity; we refer to, of course, to those [sic] ubiquitous band known as the Women's Political and Social Union, or better still, as the Militant Suffragettes.
>
> These, we have always with us now, in this country, and if it is true that, 'it's dogged that it does,' then we must admit that these undefatigable ladies [sic], are bound soon to come into their own. The suffragettes who were active in the last elections have now settled in Peterborough and are preparing to pursue their campaign in this locality with relentless vigour. We see that preparations have been made to hold a meeting on February 14 at the Corn Exchange, which will be addressed by Miss Douglas Smith, and of their cleverest speakers, and on February 22nd, Peterborough itself is to have a visit from Pankhurst who will speak in the afternoon at the Fitzwilliam Room of the Angel Hotel and in the evening at the Corn Exchange.
>
> Opinions may be bitterly opposed as to both the principle and methods of Women's Suffrage, but no-one who has ever heard of Mrs Pankhurst seems to differ as to the exceptional charm of her personality as a public speaker. Mrs Pankhurst has lately been in Paris where she had a remarkable reception amongst leading French, American and English women, her visit there ending with a highly successful meeting…she is evidently – however much we may disagree with her – one of the most remarkable of our present day celebrities, and we have no doubt that residents in both Peterborough and the adjoining districts, will take the opportunity afforded them of her visits here, to judge for themselves as to what she is and as to the merits of the cause she will lead before them.

The *Peterborough Advertiser* ran an article on this first public meeting by Pankhurst in the city with the headline: VOTES FOR WOMEN: THE SUFFRAGETTE CAMPAIGN AT PETERBOROUGH, VISIT OF MRS PANKHURST.

> When she first came to Peterborough on 22 February, (she) hosted 'at home' in the Fitzwilliam Assembly Rooms at the Angel Hotel. Mrs Mansel presided over the meeting which was attended by Katherine Clayton and her daughter Kitty, along with the Beebys who were part of the brick company of the same name, Miss Hall (principal of the Girls' High School), Nurse Wilde, and Mrs Pfleiderer (of the firm that would soon become Baker Perkins). It was said that Pankhurst was introduced as 'our leader' as she had experience of attending public meetings for over forty years and she told her audience to 'go with your patient work converting'.

Tea was served after the meeting by Helen Craggs and Miss Rowe who, in 1914, would become the local branch secretary of the National Federation of Women Workers (run by Mary McArthur, who founded the trade union body in 1906). Two notable organisers were Miss Lily Gill, the daughter of the Council's Chief Engineer, and Jessie Wadlow, daughter of a wealthy family.

Emmeline Pankhurst, the founder of the British Suffragette movement and of the Women's Social and Political Union (WSPU) paid a visit to Peterborough on 22 February 1911 to speak at the Corn Exchange on Church Street. She received a warm welcome from those who attended the event and supported her views in relation to the women's emancipation movement, which by then had been going for six years. The Peterborough Express was not so kind and used the phrase 'female hooligans' to describe the suffragettes.

> An advertisement read:
> VOTES FOR WOMEN
> A PUBLIC MEETING
> In the
> CORN EXCHANGE
> PETERBOROUGH
> ON WEDNESDAY, FEBRUARY 22ND

At 8 pm (doors open from 2.30 pm)
Speaker – MRS PANKHURST
Chair: MRS MANSEL
TICKETS 2/6 (reserved) 1/-6d. and 3d. (unreserved)
can be obtained from Miss Cragge 14 Cromwell Road
Peterborough

The building was reported to be packed on the night with women from right across the social spectrum, and some men also attended. Miss Cragge was a teacher at the County School for Girls and Mrs Mansel (from whom tickets were also available) was the chair of the district Women's and Social Political Union (WSPU).

Miss Tebbutt, a local militant suffragette, had spoken to the *Peterborough Standard* (4 March 1911) following Mrs Pankhurst's speech the previous week. She felt that the speech had 'done the cause no end of good', and that membership of the local group were slowly trickling in as the group had only just started up. Miss Tebbutt stated that members from the Peterborough area may take part in the London protests if they had no business ties on the day.

The *Peterborough Advertiser* said that the Corn Exchange meeting was crowded:

> The audience included many of the leading ladies and gentlemen of the city. The hall was profusely and artistically decorated with purple and green, and banners were suspended at intervals, bearing the mottoes of militant suffragettes. The spirit of determination which characterises the campaign of this organisation was demonstrated in such declarations as:
>
> Through thick and thin, we ne'er give in
> We fight to win
> Keep on pestering
> Arise, go forth and conquer
>
> Pankhurst was well received (and) at the end of the meeting, a vote was taken and it was almost unanimous that the room supported the latest Conciliation Bill towards Women's Suffrage.

A branch of the non-militant National Union of Women's Suffrage Societies (NUWSS) was formed in Peterborough early in 1912, and soon gained over 50 members. Miss P. English of Orton Longuville was the secretary. Campaigning was said to be busy. M.H. Renton had been working in Peterborough on the society's behalf holding two drawing room meetings; one with the Dean and another with Miss English. Ms Renton also spoke at meetings of several local organisations in preparation for a much larger meeting. On 27 February 1912, this public meeting took place at the Grand Assembly Rooms and featured Millicent Fawcett and Miss I.O. Ford, with the meeting being chaired by the Dean of Peterborough. The hall was said to be crowded with many unable to gain admittance.

Although the campaign seemed to be going well in Peterborough, strong feelings appeared in the city in regards to women gaining the vote. In 1913, the Women's Suffragist March came through Peterborough on its way between Edinburgh and London, led by Florence de Fonblanque. The march had arrived via Stamford and was met four miles outside of Peterborough by the locals. The women entered the city with banners flying high and college students followed them singing comic songs. That evening, a meeting had been arranged on Stanley Recreation Ground and was reported to have been attended by several thousand people, however, the meeting had to be broken up just ten minutes in as the crowds threw fireworks and an 'ugly' rush was made for the stage. The Suffragettes had to be escorted by the police to their hotel, the Bedford, with the crowd following, still booing and singing. The *Dundee Courier* reported Peterborough as 'being the only one (town/city) to leave any unpleasant memories' for those on the march.

The *Peterborough Advertiser* interviewed Mrs Fordham, the Honorary Secretary of the Peterborough branch of the WSPU for her opinion of the march at her 'cheery little home' in Fletton Avenue. She said 'I am thoroughly ashamed of Peterborough boys. It was not full grown and sensible citizens who rushed our meeting, threw rotten eggs and endangered life. It was not college boys either, but two to three hundred schoolboys of about fourteen years of age. And these – are the young hopefuls to be given a voice in the government of their imperial motherland. One wonders whether these mad little hooligans, these wise and chivalrous little simians, are so very much fitted when they are grown men, than women, to exercise the responsibility of the vote.' The interview concluded with 'It is interesting to record that a hat pin which Mrs Fordham was wearing on Friday night was smashed when a man seized the back of her head and attempted to twist her neck! The pin was in three pieces when home was reached and two of these were pressed into the unfortunate ladies' [sic] head. During the evening too, Mrs Fordham turned just in time to see a young girl apparently preparing to jab a long hat-pin into her back! It was altogether an exciting evening!' The *Peterborough Express* was concerned that the city could be a target of the militant suffragettes. A sentry said that the residents of Peterborough did not want them to come.

Suffrage Pilgrims read the headline of the *Peterborough Advertiser* on 16 November 1912.

RATHER SUMMARILY DEALT WITH by EXUBERANT LADS.
The tramping suffragettes in their march from Edinburgh to London, arrived in Peterborough on Friday afternoon, with their banner flying, and accompanied by roguish young men, singing humorous songs, and otherwise burlesquing what was supposedly a serious campaign to gain votes for women. Notwithstanding an official warning from the Chief Constable of the City as to the inadvisability of holding a public meeting in the Stanley Recreation Ground, the suffragettes persisted in doing so, with the result foreshadowed, that they were refused a hearing, and afterwards chased by hooligans to their headquarters at the 'Bedford' Hotel. The suffragettes left Peterborough on Saturday morning, redder and no doubt wiser women.

The suffragettes tried other methods to get the public and government's attention:

In 1913 the *Lincolnshire Echo* reported that 'Treacle Parcels' had been found in a post bag from Peterborough that had been opened in Horncastle. The act was believed to have been the work of suffragettes using a tactic of sending a jar of treacle through the post, but leaving the jar unsealed so that the contents slowly leaked all over the post in the bag.

Female hooligans were reported to be at large when, in 1913, a hoax bomb was found under the Oundle Road Railway Bridge along with a message written on the packaging stating 'Votes for Women: Handle with Care'. A further article in the Peterborough Express wrote, regarding the sentries guarding the Peterborough Cathedral: 'They do not want the suffragettes to come, but their spirit is one that says "by Jingo if they do try their little game here, there will be trouble for some of them."'

The Representation of the People Act 1918 saw British women over 30, who qualified by the type of their property, gain the vote but it was not until the Equal Franchise Act of 1928 that all women over 21 were able to vote and voting equality was achieved after roughly 100 years of campaigning.

Voluntary Aid Detachment

The women who volunteered for the VAD in Peterborough during the First World War were tireless and sympathetic in assisting Dr Jolly to look after the wounded soldiers coming through Peterborough station in hospital trains by offering refreshments and tender care. These kind ladies wore white dresses with the Red Cross emblem on their sleeves.

Dr Jolly was the commandment, Miss King the superintendent and Miss Walker the Quartermaster. These three managed the 4 sections and the 3 reservists.

Of Section A, Miss Clarabut was the leader, Lady Winfrey the cook with Miss Ball, Miss Swallow and Mrs Mackay assisting.

Of Section B, Miss Thomas was the leader, Miss Shrive the cook with Miss Farmer, Mrs Mellows, Mrs Maldrum and Mrs Hooper assisting.

Of Section C, Miss Shaw was the leader, Mrs Jolly was the cook, Miss Jolly, Miss Jessie Colman, Sister Bracewell and Miss Ruddles assisting.

Of Section D, Mrs Alec Walker was the leader, Miss Edgar was the cook, Miss Whitsed, Miss Wilkinson and Miss K.Snow were assisting.

The reserves were Mrs Morse, Mrs Ward and Miss Wilson.

On Tuesday 6 October 1914, a trainload of 108 wounded soldiers stopped for a short while at Peterborough in the early hours of the morning. Commandment Dr Jolly and the ladies from the Voluntary Aid Detachment provided soup, cake, tea and cigarettes, and care to the serious cases on board to make them more comfortable on their journey while en route to Lincoln from Southampton on the Great Northern Railway. The trains had been converted with special compartments for the soldiers and large red crosses were painted on the side panels of the train. The trains didn't bring just English soldiers back from the front, but also wounded Belgians and even Germans who were guarded in their own special carriage. By mid-December 1914, Dr Jolly reported to the Red Cross Committee that the Peterborough Voluntary Aid Detachment had assisted 1,489 soldiers who had passed through the city on the trains.

The Dogsthorpe Committee of the Red Cross Society organised a Patriotic Concert in the Dogsthorpe school at Peterborough on the evening of 21 December. The event was a musical evening with songs such as *Tipperary*, and during the interval a Miss Craig thanked everyone for attending and explained that the object of the concert was to raise money for a Christmas present to the Dogsthorpe boys who were serving in the Forces.

The mayor detailed a letter he had received in June 1916 from Sergeant O'Brien who had travelled on a Red Cross train and experienced the hospitality from Dr Jolly and the VAD team at Peterborough while passing through on his way to Lincoln:

> Dear Sir – would you kindly convey to the Red Cross Society of Peterborough the warm thanks of the patients travelling by the hospital train that passed through Peterborough yesterday evening. I am sure many a returning soldier like myself felt a wave of feeling which

> I cannot express in words at the kindness and generosity afforded us after many months of hardship. In France and Belgium, owing to the enemy's atrocities, a soldier's nature becomes savage and brutal, and his finer qualities become dormant. These finer qualities are reawakened when he returns to his homeland and sees the reception accorded him by his countrywomen and also his ineligible-for-military-service countrymen.
>
> Never did I revere my countrywomen so much as I did when I watched them in that hospital train at Peterborough. All that was good in me surged to the surface, and I thought, when I am fit to return once more to France, or wherever ordered, I will carry happy memories of Peterborough.

In July the same year, the VAD ladies were able to add St John Ambulance badges to their right arm sleeve.

Dr Jolly passed away on 8 August 1916 having made arrangements for the last time in mid-July for the next Red Cross train, gone to bed and never recovered. He was replaced by Doctor Russell Walker.

Four VAD nurses and some orderlies were sent with some wounded soldiers to an auxiliary hospital at Milton Hall where the owners, Mr. and Mrs Fitzwilliam, had provided forty beds and equipment within their Long Gallery, the Green Drawing Room, and the Reynolds Room; these wards were managed by Sister Mary of the London Hospital. The rooms still had the priceless fine art, including work by Rueben, hanging on the walls, fine silk draperies on the windows and the soldiers were able to enjoy views over the deer park. The Hall has a Georgian west front and a late Elizabethan east front, which gives the appearance of a completely different building. Additional rooms were freed up for recreation, reading, bathing and smoking. Daphne Du Maurier visited the Hall in 1917 while it was still an auxiliary hospital and has referred to this visit in her biography *Growing Pains – the Shaping of a Writer*. She was aged about 10 and visited with her mother and both sisters. It is believed that she based Manderley (from her novel *Rebecca*) on Milton Hall, as the house had made such a great impression on her.

Mr. Charles Armstrong of the depot at the Free Library made a request for all good needlewomen and knitters who were willing to give a little time to the Red Cross cause to call at the depot, which was open daily between 10.30 am to 1 pm and 2.30 pm to 5 pm. This depot was collecting for the troops of the County (approximately 12,000 men), including the 1st to the 8th Northamptonshire Regiment, the Northamptonshire Yeomanry, the local artillery Battery and some of the Hunts Cyclists.

Some women, such as Mrs B. Beckett and Mrs R. Grice, collected money towards sending tobacco for the men at the front. Parcels were dispatched to the Peterborough Yeomanry consisting of 800 quarter pounds of tobacco, 800 packets of cigarettes and 800 boxes of matches.

The mayor of Peterborough, Sir Richard Winfrey, offered accommodation, in conjunction with the city council, in Peterborough to Belgian refugees who had fled from their own country during First World War after their homeland had been over run by Germans. The first Belgian refugees arrived on 13 September 1914, with a dozen hostels opened to accommodate them. Mr. Richard Winfrey set up a Mayor's Appeal Fund raising £2,000 to help the refugees. The *Wisbech Standard* of 1914 reported that 'Over a hundred refugees have been received at Peterbro', and either housed in the city or sent into the district. Other Belgian refugees have been received at Cambridge.' Over 400 Belgians arrived in the city and local citizens made them feel so welcome that some stayed on in the area after the war ended and made permanent homes. Many families came from the Malines area and as such many were wood carvers. The Peterborough Belgian Refugee Committee helped them to start a factory in the Fletton area where they made and sold furniture. A temporary school was arranged for the fifty or so children among the refugees. Lady Margaret Proby and Miss Proby of Elton Hall offered room at their home for Belgian soldiers who had recently moved from the London Hospital. Once the war finished, many Belgians had their employment contracts terminated, and the government offered free one way tickets back to Belgium thus encouraging the Belgians to return home.

The Decorte family were housed on St Osyth's Lane in Oundle between November 1914 and 1919. The Belgian refugee project database, University of Leeds, showed that Maria Melania Decorte along with her husband Henri Josef Decorte came to Peterborough with 3 children. Three other children were subsequently born in Oundle. Maria Melania's parents were sent to Daventry some fifty miles away. Josef was employed locally as a domestic gardener.

An old picture postcard suggests that on 15 August 1914, a War Rose Day was devised in order to raise money for the Prince's War Fund. This was organised by Lady Winfrey, wife of Sir Richard Winfrey, the mayor and MP of Peterborough; at the time. Lady Winfrey was assisted by the mayoress, Mrs W.T. Mellows and a Mrs Felix Bower. They appealed for lady volunteers to meet at 3 pm. Some 2,000 roses had been donated by the florist Richard Chapman Brown of Narrow Bridge Street. The trio and their lady volunteers, all dressed in white, posed for a photograph outside the Guildhall in the city centre, and then separated to sell their flowers in the surrounding streets. At the end of the day, the group had sold over 8,000 flowers and raised more than £90 towards the fund.

War Weapons Week between 8-13 April 1918 wanted civilians to buy national war bonds priced between £5 and £5000 and war saving certificates priced between £1 and £500 so as to buy a tank which would be named after Peterborough.

The Peace Day Parade to celebrate the end of the Great War was held on 19 July 1919, with businesses, trade associations etc., such as the Peterborough Butchers Association, taking part by entering a float. A National Mission Procession was held in 1922 to promote the value of sending overseas aid.

As mentioned previously, Margaret Gibson was granted the honour of being Peterborough's first Freewoman in 1926. On 23 September the following year, the honour was awarded for the second time, going to Katharine Clayton OBE. A highly respected woman within the city, Katherine was born in 1847 and came to live in Peterborough, at the Minster Precincts, when she married the Reverend Lewis Clayton in 1872. Her husband was appointed as the Residentiary Canon at the cathedral in 1887. Katherine was not only involved with the church, she also set up the first Mothers' Union in the Diocese, as well as initiating cookery classes which she ran in local schools, the Girls' Friendly Society and the Music Festival. She was also on the inaugural committees of the Florence Saunders' Nursing Association and the Public Library. Katherine was also fascinated with another Katherine – Henry VIII's first wife, and campaigned via the newspapers to raise money through the 'Katherines of England' appeal so that a black marble slab could be placed over Katherine of Aragon's grave within the cathedral, which was done in 1895. The original slab covering her grave had been destroyed some 250 years earlier in 1643 when Oliver Cromwell's troops attacked the cathedral during the English Civil War.

The citation for Katherine's Freewoman award stated that it was given 'in recognition of the valuable public services rendered by her to the city on the numerous local government authorities and philanthropic associations with which she has been connected'. Some of the committees and associations that she had been involved with included the City Education Society, the Florence Saunders' Nursing Association, risen out of the work of the daughter of Dean Saunders, the Women and Girls' Help Society and the Peterborough Infirmary Ladies' Association. Her husband, who became Assistant Bishop of Peterborough in 1912, died in 1917, but she remained at their home in the Minster Precincts until 1927, when she moved to London and died there on 10 November in 1933, aged 90 years. She and her husband are buried together in the graveyard at the Eastern end of the cathedral.

The mayor at the start of the Second World War was Lily Violet Bryant. Ms Bryant was the first female mayor of Peterborough and 'reigned' from 1939 to 1940. Her late husband, Charles William Bryant joined Peter Brotherhood in 1902 as General Manager and they bought Westwood House in 1905, formerly residing in Charnwood on London Road. Charles was awarded the honour of Commander of the Order of the British Empire in 1917 for his service to the nation in the war, the involvement in the making of torpedo engines. Charles died on 2 March 1935 and his son, also called Charles, died six months later on 17 September, so Westwood House was sold and became a school.

Lily Bryant penned an open letter to the citizens of Peterborough which was printed in the *Standard* on the previous day; she advised everyone to prepare for any restrictions that may come into force, such as screening lighting at home and at work, street lighting restrictions had already been put into place on the 23rd. She also warned that evacuees from London would need accommodation. The Chief Constable of Peterborough, Mr Danby, also had a letter printed alongside Ms Bryant's advising that leaflets were to be distributed in relation to the new lighting and screening restrictions, and posters would be put up in regards to air-raid warning sounds.

People soon realised that the Second World War was going to be a 'Total War', with not just the armed forces being involved, but every single civilian across the country. Air-raid shelters and gun emplacements were quickly erected followed by the issue of gas masks, identification cards and ration books. On Tuesday 28 November 1939, the long awaited babies' gas masks were available for collection between 10 am and 12:30 pm, and 2pm and 4pm from the below centres:

- St John's Mission Hall on Mayor's Walk
- George Street School Room
- Congregational Church Hall in Westgate
- Cobden Street Schoolroom
- St Martin's Street First Aid Post
- Horns Street Schoolroom
- St Mary's Church Hall in St John's Street
- St Paul's Schoolroom
- Mountsteven Avenue School
- Chapel Lane Warden's Post in Werrington.

If parents couldn't make these dates then the masks were also available from the Infant Welfare Clinic in Fletton, and the Town Hall, on 30 November and 1 December at 2:30pm. Mothers had to go to the centre nearest to their home along with their identity cards in order to receive the masks. However babies living in Longthorpe and Newark had theirs delivered. Children who reached two years of age would need their mask exchanged for a larger respirator suitable for 2 to 4 years, mothers would then need to go out and acquire these extra masks.

One essential part of war work was collecting salvage of all different kinds as part of the never-ending struggle to raise money for the war effort. This was another way women on the home front could do their bit for the war. After the first appeal for salvage went out, a steady stream of stock began to be donated, from a young girl's toy tea set made of metal, to brand new aluminium goods from a gentleman's shop, as well as copper kettles and brass candlesticks. Further appeals were made at local cinemas by the mayor and Mrs Mellows. Vehicles driven by the WVS took the donated articles from the cinemas to the town hall.

The January 1941 figures for the city salvage were: Paper 34 tons, Kitchen Waste 25 tons, Milk Bottles 1,056 ,Tins 12 tons, Bones 3 tons and Ashes 5,672 tons. November 1941 salvage figures were released: Kitchen Waste 33 tons, Tins 5 tons, Bottles 101 dozen and Paper 39 tons. Within six months the total salvage tonnage of 395 tons was sold for £1,323 and yielded £188 as a bonus. The Foreman was paid £5 and £4 7s 6d was paid each to the forty-two men at the salvage department. Household waste was collected fortnightly rather than weekly due to the shortage of staff and vehicles.

A 'Bring Out Your Salvage' drive commenced on Saturday 2 May 1942, a fourteen-day attempt to achieve the collection of 137 tons of salvage – double the figure that would be normally collected in a fortnight. Householders were encouraged to donate anything they could lay their hands on as these materials were vital for the war effort; 15,000 leaflets were delivered to householders from the Ministry of Supply which carried slogans such as: 'just an old bone but it helps to bring down Heinkels'. By the evening of 13 May, the city salvage drive had reached 138 tons with three days still to go until the end of drive. Mr F.J. Smith, City engineer and surveyor issued the city's salvage figures from November 1939 to December 1944: Paper 2,620 tons, Metals 920 tons, Bones 91 tons, Kitchen Waste 1,314 tons and other materials 36,987 tons

Several hundred Belgian refugees were housed in the city during the Second World War after the Germans invaded their country. It is highly likely that their descendants remain in the city today as they were not actively encouraged to return back to Belgium after the war ceased, unlike their World War One counterparts.

The first air raid in Peterborough occurred on 6 June 1940 when six bombs were dropped near to the Soke village of Etton. Two days later, six bombs were dropped within the city itself, with one landing in Bridge Street near the current entrance of Rivergate shopping centre, another fell in Bishops Road, and one more landed in a corner tower of the Lido open air swimming pool. Later, in January 1941, the New England locomotive sheds marshalling yards experienced a German attack, with the surrounding streets of Clarence Road, St Paul's Road and Lincoln Road affected by the blast. Not long after this the cathedral became endangered when incendiary bombs landed in the vicinity of the Town Hall and the City Cinema. The city's firefighters managed to minimise the damage. During the Second World War, Peterborough experienced 644 alerts with just three people killed, nineteen injured, seven properties completely destroyed and 500 buildings damaged, so Peterborough came off very lightly to the relief of all the residents but at the same time would have been very scary for the women and children living in the streets, and the annoyance of the extra cleaning caused by the dust/debris.

Peterborough citizens also participated in a number of Fund weeks that were organised throughout the country to raise money towards the war. These funds included Wings for Victory Week, Red Army Week and Spitfire Week. In Warship week Peterborough raised around £425,000 in order to adopt the submarine HMS *Olympus* and during Spitfire Week helped fund the Spitfire No R7192.

Women's Voluntary Service

The Women's Voluntary Service (WVS) was established in 1938 by Stella Isaacs, the Marchioness of Reading, as a women's organisation to help British civilians. Across the country the WVS played an important role in helping with evacuations during the Second World War, they assisted with the collection of clothing required for the needy and assisted evacuated children with billeting. The official recruiting depot for the Civil Defence Organisations was at the Old Town Hall and was run by Mrs Margaret Mellows, wife of Arthur Mellows. She was adamant that there was a job for everyone. Because the ARP services although well equipped with personnel at the start of the war, any men under the age of 36 would soon be called up into the fighting forces so therefore their places within these voluntary organisations would need to be filled and women were ideal to fill these gaps. The WVS wore green uniforms and these became a familiar sight around Peterborough. The WVS's skills were expanded with the 'Housewife Service' in 1940. There was supposed to be a representative on every street within the city who was on hand 24 hours a day to help in the event of an air raid and to help their fellow air raid wardens and citizens and allay panic. They were trained to give treatment at home for gas casualties, to help with gas masks for babies and wore a special badge designating the role. They also had a special card displayed in their front window to show that they were prepared to turn their home into an open house should a raid occur, and would provide hot drinks, help the sick, elderly and injured.

Main requests were for people with First Aid certificates, car owners and drivers, motorcyclists to be used as dispatch drivers, stretcher bearers, clerics and people who would be willing to offer temporary accommodation to those that had been made homeless by bombing. At the end of August 1939, Mrs Margaret Mellows, in charge of the WVS appealed, on the wireless, for 200 blood donors for potential emergency blood transfusions, 200 auxiliary nurses and many women car drivers to volunteer for the service. At the same time Alderman Snowden, the chairman of the City's ARP Committee also appealed for women drivers.

Later during October in the same year, some WVS ladies as well as elementary school teachers and other ladies would help prepare the all important ration books while being supervised by the City Treasurer's Staff. By the end of the month around 90,000 ration books were ready to be distributed.

The WVS Services canteen in Market Place opened on 9 November 1939 and was manned day and night by both the WVS ladies and Toc H, Talboy House, international Christian movement.

An elaborate driving scheme and test was given to WVS driving candidates in March 1940 in the Soke of Peterborough. The trainees needed to be able to drive in the dark, to drive in a convoy, to be able to drive a lorry (in a yard, in the street, in the yard in the dark and in the street in the dark) and with trailers. Special attention would be given to the cornering and smoothness. The trainees would also be given an examination in map reading and would also be expected to work with mechanics at the Corporation's workshops.

On 9 April 1940, Mrs Margaret Mellows updated the City Council ARP meeting, chaired by Alderman Snowden, stating that she now had a total of 1,425 WVS ladies enrolled onto her books and that each of these women were ready for any kind of emergency that should occur. The WVS ladies covered a number of departments including ambulance drivers and attendants, evacuation duties, first aiders supplementing the St John's Ambulance workers, service canteen workers, transport drivers, clerical workers in First Aid Posts (FAP) and working within a panic squad. The WVS working within a panic squad would only be needed if there was a significant raid. In the event of one occurring between 60 and 100 WVS ladies would look after newly homeless people within 3 large halls spread across the town and specially earmarked for the purpose, for approximately 48 hours.

The WVS volunteers took part in the first full ARP test mobilization for the North Midland Defence Region on Sunday, 5 May 1940. Official umpires from nearby neutral towns made observations and reported to the Regional Office on how well they found the exercise went – conclusion was well satisfied. During the Peterborough test 124 bombs had been dropped in the town causing 68 deaths and 137 injuries. The younger women of the Women's Voluntary Service along with the Boy

Scouts played some of the roles of the injured during this 'test' raid.

The ladies of the WVS at the end of May/beginning of June 1940 took on a new role of meeting the British Expeditionary Force troop trains so as to arrange refreshments for the armed forces. Railway trolleys were placed all along the platforms serving biscuits, buns, cakes and lemonade. Each time a train pulled up there was a sea of khaki. The ladies also gave out cigarettes and postcards, many of which they posted on behalf of the soldiers as this was the first chance many soldiers had to contact their loved ones. The WVS were kept constantly on their toes as new trains would arrive every twenty minutes and teacups needed washing!

During this time, the WVS was asking for old mattresses, no matter what their condition. These mattresses would be fixed onto the top of ambulances and cars to be used as protection against shrapnel. Mrs Mellows could arrange collection of any mattresses that could be donated to the organisation.

In the Precincts could be found the Women's Services Canteen which was established in August 1940 and was very popular thanks to its beds, books, baths and tea room.

In the second week of October 1940, the 3 WVS officers for the Fletton Urban District Council – Mrs Atkinson, Mrs Morley Wells and Mrs Allen – helped with the compulsory billeting of evacuated mothers and children. The ladies obtained and handed out toys, and clothing; mainly woollies, pullovers and overcoats. Approximately 1,000 official evacuees arrived from London on 11 October. After alighting the train, mothers and children were taken from the train station to the Salvation Army Citadel where a hot meal was waiting for them. Outside the church in King's Street was a spread of bags, parcels and trunks. The WVS took the pre-arranged groups by car to their individual billets

At the end of November 1940, it was decided by the Civil Defence Organisations that the provision for rest centres and emergency feeding should be increased from three centres to seventeen based on raid experiences elsewhere in Britain. Large stocks of articles required for each centre were parceled out to each individual centre by the WVS. A request was issued to residents that in order to help with the rescue, should properties be bombed, that each household should put up a notice, outside their house or on their front gate, stating how many people were sleeping in the property so that rescue and first aid properties knew how many people to deal with. By the end of January 1941, the Public Assistance Committee had decided that the WVS should organise and run these rest centres with volunteers placed on shifts ready to spring into action should an emergency occur.

The centres in the city were:

- St Margaret's Church Hall in Fairfield Road
- Methodist Schoolroom in Wentworth Street
- Barrass Memorial Hall in Park Road
- Werrington Church Hall in Palmerston Road
- Werrington C of E School in Werrington
- King's School in Park Road
- Methodist Schoolroom in New England
- St Mary's Church Hall in St John's Street
- Haig Memorial Hall in Brook Street
- Deacon's School in Deacon's Street

The centres in the rural areas around the city were:

- Barnack C of E School
- Thornhaugh Council School
- Castor and Ailsworth War Memorial Hall
- Eye C of E Senior School
- Peakirk Parish Hall
- Helpston Council School

Also in December 1940 the WVS were appealing for motorcycle dispatch riders as other towns had discovered that if telegraphic communications become damaged then a backup service that is readily available is essential. Petrol would be supplied and the City Engineer would provide the necessary equipment needed.

Enrolment through the usual Old Town Hall office of Margaret Mellows. The same lady also made a request for old gloves so that they could be used in rescue parties to deal with broken glass and also unpleasant jobs. By 1941 Mrs Mellows had over 3,000 members of the WVS in Peterborough.

During the months of April and May in 1941, Mrs Mellows ran four sessions of lectures on how to handle a gas situation. These talks, held at the town hall on 22 April, 29 April, 6 May and 13 May were aimed mainly at wives of active servicemen living in the city and followed the receipt of a Ministry of Home Security circular regarding the wearing of gas masks. The lectures covered dealing with incendiary bombs and fires, protecting yourself during such a situation, first aid for any casualties and the latest available information about gas attacks. Over 450 ladies turned up to the very first lecture and those that attended all four lectures would receive a Women's Voluntary Service badge.

In June 1941, the WVS helped with placing food into storage should emergency feeding arrangements need activating for 6,000 residents. Adults would be charged 6d and children under 10 4d. The WVS mobile canteens could supplement the service, at the seven schools which were designated as potential emergency feeding centres:

- Walton Senior
- New Fletton
- West town Junior Mixed
- Eastholm Infants
- Cromwell Road Mixed & Infants
- Lincoln Road Girls
- Fulbride Junior

The National Savings Committee asked the Women's Voluntary Service to help organise street groups within the city. Out of a total of 276 streets, between March 1941 and August 1941, 254 had been visited by the ladies working on behalf of the WVS.

By December 1941, there were another five service canteens in the city for the Armed Forces which were working to capacity every day with discussions being opened with the railway authorities about opening a further canteen at Peterborough East station. The three WVS mobile canteens – Louis D, Baker Perkins and Anne Norris – attended to army forces who required their services at out-of-the-way camps, no matter what the weather. The ARP decided to purchase a mobile canteen for their own use and asked if the WVS would mind staffing it. The Town Clerk also applied for an American Red Cross canteen, located in Northamptonshire, to be used in the Soke and be staffed accordingly.

Following the second anniversary of the start of the Second World War there was a big recruitment drive to fill in the gaps in the defence services as the end was not looking near. The WVS still needed another 200 auxiliary nurses as well as many women car drivers as could be found. Forward on to the beginning of January 1941 and the WVS was now looking for more helpers for their canteens. Due to the call-up of women, the WVS needed assistance at Long Causeway on a Tuesday between 9 and 11 am as well as night helpers between 11 pm and 7 am on Saturdays, Sundays and Mondays. The mobile canteens also needed drivers even if it was just one shift a week or a fortnight.

In March 1942, rest centre exercises were held at:

- Palmerston Road Church Hall in Woodston, run by Mrs Atkinson
- St Margaret's Hall in Fairfield Road, run by Mrs Laxton and Mrs Smith
- King's School, run by Mrs Shearcroft
- Castor, run by the Honourable Mrs Pelham
- Werrington, run by Mrs Kirman

The intention was to hold exercises at all of the rest centres within both the City and the Soke of Peterborough. Rest centres catered for those that had been made homeless due to enemy action and as such volunteers, mainly school children, were needed to replicate potential injuries, or problems such as 'hysteria' and lost relations.

Another seventy WVS members assisted with a further practice exercise in the city. Exercise Delta was carried out on 21 and 22 November 1942. The exercise was designed to assess how Peterborough's civilians and military/civil defence services would cope and react to a heavy air attack and an invasion attempt. Mrs Mellows, the County Organiser for the WVS reported on how the suddenly homeless would be provided for in such a scenario with buildings commandeered to house those affected. All in all, Exercise Delta was reported to be a success, although some minor injuries were incurred and a few personnel stood too close to the 'enemy'.

At the beginning of 1943, it was announced that Peterborough had been allocated seven tanks through the Tanks for Attack campaign run by the National Savings Committee and one tank was named the Peterborough WVS Street Groups.

In mid-July 1944, although several thousand evacuees had already been billeted in Peterborough and the surrounding areas, there were still some evacuees arriving unexpectedly and placing a strain on both the Peterborough billeting authorities and the WVS. On this occasion Woodston Church in Palmerston Road had to be opened as a rest centre with Mrs Atkinson of the WVS organising the staffing arrangements. Midday dinner was served at the British restaurant and the WVS served the other meals. The evacuees stayed for a week while both the council billeting team and the WVS attempted to find the mothers and children accommodation, which proved a challenge if they were a mother with six children who did not wish to be split up. Some evacuees ended up being relocated to other parts of the country as there was simply a lack of accommodation locally.

In April 1945, the Army Welfare Officer at Peterborough asked (the) WVS to operate a 'Get You Home Scheme' so that men on leave from overseas who were stranded at the stations at night could be taken home by car.

Women's Land Army

Mrs S.G. Cook was the local representative for the Women's Land Army in May 1940. The Women's Land Army was experiencing a slow response to their recruiting campaign in comparison to the other organisations recruiting at this time. Most girls who volunteered were untrained and training now had to be completed on the job rather than at a college due to the urgency of positions to be filled. Later, on the second anniversary of the start of the war, Mrs Cook was able to report that she'd had a better influx of candidates following a big drive to fill the gaps in the civil defence organisations. In July 1942 there were 110 Women's Land Army volunteers in the Soke of Peterborough; 106 of these were employed and 4 were receiving training. The girls were either living on the farms they were working on or in Barnack or Newborough Hostels, which could house 26 women each. Sacrewell Farm was a leading battery hen farm during the Second World War, the young farm workers were drafted into the war leaving the land unfarmed so William Abbott and his wife Mary acquired some Land Army girls to help. Sacrewell Farm was a radical farming centre with intense production of food and dairy and was a saviour food-wise for the local area. However by 1948 Mr. Abbott's hen and dairy stocks were much depleted and rationing was now in full flow. Many girls came to Castor and Ailsworth to work on the farms, they helped with ploughing, harvesting and with milking the cows. Some of these girls married local men and made their homes in the villages.

In June 1943, three young ladies from the Women's Land Army in the Peterborough area were fined £1 for writing love letters to Italian prisoners, who were also working on the land. The man who delivered the letters on their behalf, described in court as a wounded war hero, was also fined.

By 1942, girls aged 17 or older were also expected to join the boys in giving up their leisure time and either join a youth organisation, or participate in Civil Defence work. Youth organisers in March 1942 sifted through the registration cards for this age group and interviewed all concerned.

Girls who were aged 20 on 19 April 1941 were required to register. These girls were required to bring their registration cards, which a fair few forgot to bring. Leaflets were handed out explaining the different services available, e.g. the WAAF (Women's Auxiliary Air Force), WRNS, and nursing. Many girls came with their mothers or aunts for support and a few arrived with an army escort beside them. Peggy from Ailsworth joined the Auxiliary Territorial Service in 1940 and ended up in barracks at Barnard Castle. The ATS became the Number 6 Training Centre for permanent staff to train 1,000 conscripted girls for their initial training – kitting them out in uniforms, doing drills, gas lectures, PT and route marches.

War Weapons Week began on Saturday 30 November 1940, with both British and German exhibits on display in Market Place. The WAAF and airmen demonstrated the exhibits where necessary, which included incendiary bomb baskets, portable oxygen apparatus and Browning machine guns as well as a German Luftwaffe bomber which was on display at the King's School for members of the public and pupils to view closely at the cost of 15 shillings. By the end of the week nearly £450,000 had been raised towards buying the Navy a destroyer – £100,000 over the initial target.

An ambulance was gifted to the city of Peterborough from the people of the town of Peterborough in New Hampshire, United States of America. This was accepted in a ceremony that was held in the Market Place on Thursday 26 June, 1941. A Mrs Somerville-Smith from the British-American Ambulance Corps presented the ambulance to the Duchess of Gloucester, who received it on behalf of the city's residents. Both the Union Jack and the Stars and Stripes were crossed behind the platform, which was flanked by both plants and plant pots borrowed from Central Park greenhouses, and the national flags were also flying from the facade of the town hall. In the square were members of the ARP Units, the Women's Voluntary Services, 400 members of the 1st Peterborough City Battalion, the Home Guard under Lieutenant Colonel R.J.C. Crowden MC, the Commanding Officer. The ambulance itself was standing in front of the gates memorial fountain.

A Violet Hilda Parker of 59 Harris Street was accused of stealing from the North Station Canteen. She was charged with stealing a bottle of coffee of the value of 4 shillings on or about 21 January, and also the taking of 5*s* 6*d* in cash on or about 11 February. These items were the property of Margaret Mellows and other members of the WVS. Mrs Parker assisted at the canteen and was occasionally in charge of the shift there. She had admitted to Constable Unsworth that she had been tempted to steal, having seen others do the same, and had asked the Constable to accept £2 in restitution. The Chief Constable stated that both Mrs Parker and her husband were respectable people with two children and held a good position; there was no need for Mrs Parker to steal. The chairman stated that the case was more than distressing because the defendant was masquerading on public service when she had pinched the money. If others were doing it too, then they should feel ashamed. Mrs Parker was fined £2 10*s* on each charge.

Miss D.M. Field, a local lass, was mentioned in the paper on 22 February; she was serving as a matron on the Arakan front in Burma. Miss Field had lived in Peterborough most of her life and had been taught at All Saints School, she then went on to train as a nurse at both Northampton General and Edinburgh Royal Hospitals.

A newspaper reporter writing a few days previous said:

> When the Seventh Indian Division on the far side of the Mayu Ridge is relieved, the wounded will find British nurses waiting to tend to them. These nurses – there are only five of them so far – are the first women to serve right up at the Arakan front in this campaign or any other. And they are the only white women within 120 miles of Chittagong, whence they arrived last night, aching with weariness after bumping over hot, dusty roads. Early this morning they were at work in casualty clearing stations in the neighbourhood of Bawii Bazaar, a village a few miles north of the Ngakyedauk Pass, over which the wounded will be brought out. From down the road came the thud of mortar bombs and the crash of shells. The nurses took no notice; they just carried on, living up to the name they have already given themselves, 'the most forward women in Arakan'. They were just sitting down to a meal of

bully and beans in their hill-top mess tent, overlooking the Naaf River, when I met them. Their Matron, Miss D.M. Field, of Peterborough, spent seven years nursing in Burma, and marched out the hard way with our troops and the refugees when we withdrew to India. Now, with three pips on her shoulders, she has returned to nurse the men on the Arakan front because she thinks it will help our wounded if they have a woman's care and attention, immediately they come back from the line.

Another statistical fact – by 4 July 1942, 564 women from Peterborough who had registered for national service had been born in 1900.

The Fire Watching statistics for October 1942 showed that almost 9,000 women had registered for duty and approximately 900 men. However, 65 per cent of women aged 20–45 and 90 per cent of men aged 18–60 had claimed exemption. The reasons women gave for claiming exemption were that they needed to provide care for children under the age of 14 (it was required to give the children's national registration number in order to claim exemption), they already had long working hours, or were already on fire watching duties. The Fire Guard was the largest department of Civil Defence and volunteers numbered over 5,000,000. Fire Watching competitions were held and on 9 July 1943, Group Five (East Ward), which was represented by Miss N. Wright (Captain), Miss J. Relph and Miss V. Johnson, won the Corey Fire Guard Cup at the town park. The runners up were also an all female team, group 8.

Afterword

Peterborough as a quickly growing city has had a number of interesting female residents from the brave nurse Edith Cavell to the potential Jack the Ripper victim Alice McKenzie. Each of these women's stories are just as fascinating as the next. Women's lives during this period in Peterborough rose and fell perhaps more quickly than in some other areas with the opportunities such as war work making munitions and fixing war vehicles, as well as the Women's Land Army and simply just replacing the men in their every day jobs only for them to return from the war and the women having to resume 'women's work'. There was also a mixed response from the city's residents as to the women's right to vote with the great pilgrimage receiving an unusual welcome to Emmeline Pankhurst's speeches with an overwhelming consensus on the view of the Conciliation Bill. If you visit the Cathedral, do be sure to stop by Katharine of Aragon's tomb and Edith Cavell's memorial, and spend a few moments thinking about the brave women of the city.

Abigail

Bibliography

Bates, D. (2016). *Historical research using British newspapers* Barnsley: Pen & Sword History.

Brandon, D. and Knight, J. (2001). *Peterborough past: the City and the soke* Chichester: Phillimore.

Bridger, G. and Barnett, C. (2013). *The Great War Handbook* Barnsley: Pen & Sword Family History.

Bull, J. and Bull, V. (1988). *Peterborough* Loggerheads: S.B. Publications.

Bull, J. and Bull, V. (2018). *Secret Peterborough* Stroud: Amberley Publishing.

Bull, J. and Bull, V. (2013). *Peterborough then & now* Stroud: The History Press.

Bull, J. and Bull, V. (2011). *Peterborough through time* Stroud: Amberley.

Carradice, P. (2014). *An illustrated introduction to the First World War* Stroud: Amberley.

Gray, D. (2008). *No more strangers : a record of Peterborough men killed during First World War* Peterborough: David Patrick Gray.

Gray, D. (2014). *Peterborough at War, 1914–1918* Great Britain: David Patrick Gray.

Gray, D. (2011). *Peterborough at War, 1939–1945* Peterborough: David Patrick Gray.

Hattersley, R. (2009). *Borrowed time: the story of Britain between the wars* London: Abacus.

Hooper, J. (2012). *Peterborough* Stroud: The History Press.

Jones, B. (2014). *The Peterborough book of days* Stroud: The History Press.

Lewis, J. (2014). *A brief history of World War I* London: Robinson.

Liquorice, M. (1991). *Posh folk* Peterborough: Cambridgeshire Libraries Publications.
Mackreth, D. (1994). *Peterborough*. Dover, N.H.: Alan Sutton.
McKenzie, R. (2007). *A hundred years of Baker Perkins at Westwood Works 1903–2003* Peterborough: Baker Perkins Historical Society.
Muir, A. (1968). *The History of Baker Perkins.* Peterborough: Heffer.
Newby, J. (2011). *Women's lives: researching women's social history, 1800–1939* Barnsley: Pen & Sword Books Ltd.
People of Peterborough Vol 2: *More famous, infamous & interesting people [etc]*. (2011). Peterborough: Peterborough Publications.
Pugh, M. (2009). *We danced All Night* London: Vintage.
Shared learning Members, P. (2008). *People of Peterborough. Famous, infamous & interesting people from the history of Peterborough* (Volume 1) Peterborough: Peterborough Museum Collections.
Shared learning Members, P. (2009). *People of Peterborough. Famous, infamous & interesting people from the history of Peterborough* (Volume 2) Peterborough: Peterborough Museum Collections.
Souhami, D. (2010). *Edith Cavell* London: Quercus Publishing.
Tebbs, H. (1979). *Peterborough* Cambridge: Oleander Press.

Newspapers

Peterborough Advertiser
Peterborough Standard
The Police Gazette

Archives

Cambridgeshire Archives
Peterborough Archive Service
Peterborough Museum
The Peterborough Tea Room Books

Websites

Commonwealth War Graves: cwgc.org
dailymail.co.uk/news/article-2119338/The-donkey-born-First-World-War-trench-mascot-British-troops.html
eyepeterborough.co.uk
findagrave.com
peterboroughww1.co.uk/peterborough-druring-world-war-1
peterboroughimages.co.uk
peterboroughtoday.co.uk/news/environment/in-focus-the-women-who-made-our-city-what-it-is-today-1-57809
peterborough-cathedral.org.uk
thegazette.co.uk
vad.redcross.org.uk/Volunteers-during-WW1
womenslandarmy.co.uk
womenwhoshapedpboro.wordpress.com/category/florence-saunders
www2.westsussex.gov.uk/learningresources/LR/effects_of_rationing_on_the_home_fronte4bf.pdf

Index

Accident, 26, 53, 66, 77
Ailsworth, 11, 79, 108, 112, 113
Air raid, 43, 45–7, 50–1, 69, 104–105
  shelters, 46–7, 50–1, 69
Alderman, Edith, 76
Almshouse, *Intro*, 59–60
Americans, 37, 49–50, 85, 91, 110, 113
Angel Hotel 5, 41, 78–9, 81, 91–2
Ashworth, Elizabeth, *see* Rist, Betsey
Ashworth, John, 55–6
Asylum, 56
Auxiliaries, 23, 30, 33–4, 52, 98, 105, 110, 113

Baker Perkins, 24, 92, 110
Bassett, Annie, 74–5
Belgian families, 18, 97, 99–100, 104
Benstead, Gladys, 4
Birth, 21, 33, 63, 67
Bishop, 4–5, 15, 16, 86–9, 101
Bishop's Palace, 52, 62
Bishops Road, 46, 69, 104

Bodger's Yard, 44
Bombs, 8, 50, 104, 106, 109, 114
Boongate, 6, 65, 68
Brickyards, 27, 28
Bridge Fair, 44, 80–1, 86
Bryant, Lily Violet, 101–102

Castor, 3, 11, 30, 48, 79, 108, 110, 112
Cathedral, 1–6, 12, 15–16, 37, 39, 46, 50, 60, 73–5, 87, 96, 101, 104
Cavell, Edith, 1–2, 16
Celta, 31–2
Census, 21–2, 24, 55–6, 58
Central Park, 72–3, 113
Christmas, 49, 52–3, 58–9, 79, 81, 89, 97
Church, 3, 10–12, 16–17, 19, 29, 39, 41–2, 66, 73, 87, 89, 92, 101–102, 107–108, 110–11
Civilian Repair Unit, 36
Clayton, Katherine, 4–5, 75, 92, 100
Colman, 27
Corn Exchange, 49, 52, 88, 91–3

Cottage homes, 59
Cowgate, 10, 42, 50, 61
Craggs, Helen, 90, 92
Creighton, Louise, 5
Cumbergate, *Intro*, 59, 60

Dispensary, 51, 61
Dogsthorpe, 12, 24, 42, 72, 97
Domestic abuse, 69–70
Domestic service, 21, 23, 27

Education, *Intro*, 5, 9–20, 101
Electric, 25, 29, 40, 42–3, 47–8, 72
Employment, 20–37
Employment Exchange, 33–5
Evacuees, 47–8, 102, 107, 111

Farrow, 26–8, 47
Fashion, 22, 38–9
Fengate, 51, 69
Fitzwilliam, 11, 30, 39, 51, 58, 63, 68, 73, 81, 91–2, 98
Fletton, 26–9, 42, 46–7, 50, 52, 68, 74, 85, 94, 99, 102, 107, 109
Floods, 44
Food, 39–41, 45
Frederick Sage, 24, 30
Freewoman, 15, 75, 100–101
Frothblowing, 78–9

Gable, Clark, 85
Gibson, Margaret, 1, 6, 15–16, 100
Glyn, Lady Mary, 88–9

Hill, John Cathles, 24, 29
  Matilda, 24
  May, 16
Hodgson, Lily, 7–8
Horse bus, 42, 71
Horsey Toll, 36
Hospital, 1, 6–8, 30–1, 47, 49, 51–3, 56–7, 61–3, 68, 78, 84, 89, 96–9, 114
Housing, 28–9, 41–2

Infant welfare, 68, 102
Infirmary, *Intro*, 6–7, 51–2, 57, 60–2, 67, 101
Influenza, 61

Jack the Ripper, 64, 66
Jolly, Dr, 60, 67, 96–8
Jubilee, 73–4

Katherine of Aragon, 2–3, 101
Kesteven, *see* Asylum

Land army, 31, 33, 112
Laurel Court, 1–2, 6, 15–16
Lincoln Road, 11, 17, 41, 42, 72–3, 77, 84, 87, 104, 109
London Brick Company, 28
Long Causeway, 52, 61, 63, 81, 110
Low Farm, 51, 62
Lunatics, 61

Mc Cormack, 65–6
McKenzie, Alice, 63–6

Market, 30, 39–40, 46, 53, 71, 73, 81–2, 89, 106, 113
Mary Queen of Scots, 4, 37
Maternity, 47, 52, 63
Maurier, Daphne du, 98
Mayor, 4, 10, 15, 37, 45, 47, 49, 53, 68, 73–4, 85–6, 88, 97, 99–101, 103
Mellows, Margaret, 96, 103, 105–107, 109, 111, 114
Memorial, 1, 3, 5, 14, 35, 46, 49, 51, 54, 62–3, 84, 108, 113
Milton, 11, 30, 47, 52, 58, 61, 98
Miss Pear, *Intro*, 59–60
Munitions, 22, 30, 33, 35
Murder, 63–7
Museum, 50–1, 62

National Union of Women's Suffrage Societies (NUWSS), 94
Nene, 42, 44, 72
New England, 11, 41, 46, 60, 71, 78, 84, 104, 108
New Fletton, 25, 28–9, 109
New Road, 11, 42, 87

Operating theatre, *Intro* 51

Pankhurst, Emmeline, 5, 90–3
Pantiles, 29
Park Road, 16–17, 29, 81, 108
Perkins, 24, 30, 92, 110
Peterborough Advertiser, 7, 10, 28, 30, 38–9, 53, 61, 63, 67, 74–5, 80, 91–5
Peterborough, East, 42, 110
Peterborough, North, 49
Peterborough, Standard, 14, 23–4, 29, 33, 38, 49, 52, 58–9, 63, 68, 76, 78, 87, 89, 93, 102
Peter Brotherhood, 24, 30, 101
Peterscourt, 13–14
Police, 49, 64, 66–7, 69, 94
Poor Law, 56–9, 61
Post Office, 9, 11, 17, 24, 34, 49
Priestgate, *Intro*, 42, 50–1, 62, 71
Prostitution, 21, 55, 64–5

Railway, 4, 7, 11, 14, 27, 29–30, 39, 41–3, 46–7, 60, 62–3, 71, 73, 80, 84, 89, 96–7, 107, 110
  Great Eastern, 42, 89
  Great Northern, 41–2, 84, 97
  London, 42
  Midland, 4, 42, 73
Rally, 30
Rationing, 4, 26, 50, 52, 102, 106, 112
Red Cross, 17, 50, 52, 61, 96–9, 110
Rist, Betsey, 55–6
Roberts, Katherine, 75–6

Salvage, 103
Saunders, Florence, 6–7, 10
School,
   British, 10–13
   County School, 17–19, 93
   Dame, *Intro*, 9
   Deacon's, 9, 108
   Elementary, 9–13, 17, 105
   High School for Girls, 16–17, 92
   Laurel Court, *see* Laurel Court
   National Society, 10–13
   Workhouse, 14–15
Sedan Chair, 71
Servants, 22–4, 41, 60, 67
Slipper Baths, 46, 51
Smallpox, 51, 60, 62
Star Pressed Brick Company, 24
St John Ambulance, 35, 98, 106
St John's (Church), 12, 66, 73
St John's (hospital), 47, 49, 52, 57
St Mark's, 11–12
St Mary's, 11, 73, 102, 108
St Peter's, 13–14, 17–18
Strickland, 10
Suffrage, 4–5, 89–96
Sutton, 11, 62, 79
Swimming, 18, 50, 72, 104
Symington, 25–8

Tebutt, Miss, 93
Temperance, 86–9
Theatres, 39, 76, 81–4
Tram, 42–3, 72
Transport, 41–3, 106
Thorpe Road, *Intro*, 18, 49, 56, 57, 63, 73

Upton, 11, 30

Vagrancy, 55–7, 68–9
Van Dissel, Annette, 6, 15–16
Voluntary Aid Detachment (VAD), 30, 96–8

Walton, 30, 41–3, 47, 72, 109
War Rose Day, 100
War Weapons Week, 100
Weddings, 32, 41, 75
Werner Pfeiderer & Perkins, *see* Perkins
Werrington, 12, 43, 102, 108, 110
Westgate, 11, 42
Westwood, 30
Whittlesey, 24
Whitwell, Elizabeth & Susannah, 9
   John, 9, 14, 61
Women's Auxiliary Air Force, 33, 113
Women's Social and Political Union (WSPU), 90–3
Women's Suffragist March, 94–5
Women's United Total Abstinence Council (WUTAC), 87–9

Women's Voluntary Service (WVS), 33, 48, 50, 53, 103–111, 113–14
Woodston, 12, 26, 28, 42, 84, 110–11
Wood Street, 11, 54, 72, 90, 102

Workhouse, *Intro*, 6, 14–15, 52, 56–9, 60, 63, 68–9, 74
Union, 56–8, 61

Yaxley, 43, 55